GRAND CANYON
NATIONAL
MONUMENT

Kanab Creek

Tapeats Creek

GREAT THUMB
MESA

Chikapanagi Point

Towago Point

Colorado River

POWELL PLATEAU

Havasu Creek

HAVASUPAI
INDIAN
RESERVATION

GRANITE GORGE

Shinumo

Apache Point

TRAIL

Havasupai Point

Hualapai Hilltop

Hopi Point

Powell Memorial

Mohave Point

Yavapai Point

TRAIL

Yavapai Museum

Mather Point

COCONI

BRIGHT ANGEL TRAIL

EAST RIM DRIVE

WEST RIM DRIVE

D
Te

Park Headquarters
Visitor Center

TRAIL

Railroad Station

Shrine of
the Ages

Yavapai Lodge

GRAND CANYON
VILLAGE
Visitor Center

Parking

Post
Office

Trailer Village

Motor
Lodge

Service

Campground

Maintenance

Hospital

Morris

0   ½   1 MILE

Grand Canyon National Park

MARBLE CANYON NATIONAL MONUMENT

NAVAJO INDIAN RESERVATION

PRIMITIVE ROAD

KAIBAB PLATEAU

MARBLE GORGE

Point Imperial

Mount Hayden

Nankoweap Creek

Vista Encantadora

Kwagunt Creek

Bright Angel Point

Gunther Castle

Atoko Point

Little Colorado R.

WALHALLA PLATEAU

Cape Solitude

Shiva Temple

Buddha Temple

Isis Temple

Deva Temple

Angels Window

PAINTED DESERT

Bright Angel Creek

KAIBAB TRAIL

Brahma Temple

Venus Temple

Cape Royal

Zoroaster Temple

Wotan's Throne

Apollo Temple

Phantom Ranch

FOOT BRIDGE

Vishnu Temple

GRANITE RAPIDS

KAIBAB TRAIL

GRANITE GORGE

Vishnu Creek

Comanche Point

Monument Creek

Pima Point

Hopi Point

Cedar Mountain

Hermits Rest

GRAND CANYON VILLAGE

Yaki Point

Colorado River

Watchtower

Visitor Center

Lipan Point

Tusayan Museum

Grandview Point

Moran Point

0   5   10
MILES

The Magnificent West: GRAND CANYON

Also by Milton Goldstein

The Magnificent West: YOSEMITE

The Magnificent West:
GRAND CANYON

By Milton Goldstein
With 60 Photographs in Color

Doubleday & Company, Inc., Garden City, New York

Glossary of Geologist's and Naturalist's Terms (updated
by Milton Goldstein) from A GUIDE TO THE NATIONAL PARKS
By William H. Matthews, III.
Copyright © 1968, 1973 by William H. Matthews, III.
Used by permission of Doubleday & Company, Inc.

Library of Congress Cataloging in Publication Data

Goldstein, Milton, 1915–
      The magnificent West, Grand Canyon.

      Bibliography: p. 189
      Includes index.
      1. Grand Canyon.   I. Title.
F788.G57   917.91′3
                    ISBN 0-385-11030-8
Library of Congress Catalog Card Number: 75-40158
          Copyright © 1977 by Milton Goldstein
                  All rights reserved
          Printed in the United States of America
                     First Edition

To My Beloved Daughter

JALONA

Lovely, Wise,
Sensitive, Intense,

Whose Beautiful Soul
and
Creative Talents
Have Enriched My Life

Preface

IN this book I have tried to express the love and worship—without which life would have no meaning for me—inspired in me by the grandest of all canyons. Like John Muir, "I have done my best to show forth the beauty, grandeur . . . with a view to inciting the people to come and enjoy them, and get them into their hearts."

Creating my pictures is a solitary act—total absorption in my vision excludes the rest of the world: no one else exists for me, and even the surrounding landscape disappears.

But selecting the pictures for the book and writing the text are essentially social—attempts to share my feelings with those who love the mountains, and those who would if given the chance.

Reflecting on my Grand Canyon visions at this time has been a moving experience for me. A recent encounter with death has led me to a re-examination of the basic values of my life, and nothing speaks so eloquently to me of life and death and the enduring values by which we live as does the most awesome of all visual experiences—the Grand Canyon.

Reviewing my pictures has revealed to me that a moment of transcendent beauty is a joy forever, enshrined in the heart.

Contents

LIST OF THE PHOTOGRAPHS

I INTRODUCTION

Introduction

THE Grand Canyon is the essence of a world too large to grasp, too complex to comprehend, and too strange to feel at home in. "This is God's world, not man's," it thunders.

Were the Grand Canyon merely one canyon, it would be impressive, with its vast and steep vistas. But what gives the Grand Canyon its overwhelming impact is the fantastic complexity of architecture, light, shadow, and color—all culminating in an infinite variety of patterns of beauty.

Solitude and silence, values increasingly ignored in the frenzy for togetherness and noise, are revived here as fundamentals of the human spirit, refreshing the weary and healing the hurt, turning infidels into believers and believers into prophets.

The Grand Canyon is an awesome spectacle of transcendent beauty, offered by Nature to all who love her. One's favorite temples, stunningly arrayed in configurations of rich color and striking form, are resonant chords in the heart of man, fulfilling his hunger for magnificence.

The spectacular vistas of the Grand Canyon are not merely wonders to dazzle the eye, they are also invitations to the heights and depths of human experience.

The extremes of response to the overwhelming Canyon scene where dramatically expressed by a storyteller called Fitz-Mac over seventy years ago:

> It is at once the most awful and the most irresistible thing I have ever beheld. It is a paradox of chaos and repose, of gloom and radiance, of immeasurable desolation and enthralling beauty. It is a despair and a joy; a woe and an ecstasy; a requiem and a hallelujah; a world-ruin and a world-glory . . .

The religious feeling of many viewers was depicted by another early visitor, William Winter:

> A pageant of ghastly desolation and yet of frightful vitality, such as neither Dante nor Milton in their most sublime conceptions ever even approached. . . . Your heart is moved with feeling that is far too deep for words. Hour after hour you would sit, entranced, at the edges of this mighty subterranean spectacle, lost in the wonder and glory of it, forgetful of self, and conscious only of the Divine Spirit.

And the colorful heart of the Canyon was described by the famous editor William Allen White:

> Here at this Canyon, the sun and the dry, clear air are painting a changing picture, full of color, full of the spirit of motion, full of mystery. One should not say that the canyon is beautiful; it transcends mere beauty and passes into a "far more exceeding glory."
>
> But the heart of it is color. It is a rhapsody in color—great splashes and bands and daubs of color—blue shadows, deep and dead, tawny, strawberry-tinged layers of granite; all the yellows in the paintbox; greens and gray-greens and pinks and lavenders, and half-tones floating on the sun wraiths that haunt the air. He who can look at this monster chasm and not feel his soul stirring in uncanny sympathy with its depth is dead, and Gabriel's trumpet will do little for him.

John Muir, enthusiastic celebrant of the beauties of Yosemite and the Sierra Nevada, also loved the Canyon. In recommending in 1901 that it be designated a national park (accomplished in 1919), he paid tribute to its grandeur:

> The Grand Canyon Reserve of Arizona, of nearly two million acres, of the most interesting part of it, should be made into a national park, on account of its supreme grandeur and beauty. Setting out from Flagstaff, on the way to the Canyon, you pass through beautiful forests of yellow pine and curious dwarf forests of nut pine and juniper. After riding or walking seventy-five miles through these pleasure-grounds, the San Francisco and other mountains, abounding in flowery parklike openings and smooth shallow valleys with long vistas which in fineness of finish and arrangement suggest the work of a consummate landscape artist . . . you come to the most tremendous Canyon in the world. It is abruptly countersunk in the forest plateau, so that you see nothing of it until you are suddenly stopped on its brink, with its immeasurable wealth of divinely colored and sculptured buildings before you and beneath you. No matter how far you have wandered hitherto, or how many famous gorges and valleys you have seen, this one, the Grand Canyon of the Colorado, will seem as novel to you, as unearthly in the color and grandeur and quantity of its architecture, as if you had found it after death, on some other planet; so incomparably lovely and grand and supreme is it above all the other canyons in our fire-molded, earthquake-shaken, rain-washed, wave-washed, river- and glacier-sculptured world. It is about six thousand feet deep where you first see it, and from rim to rim ten to fifteen miles wide. Instead of being dependent for interest upon waterfalls, depth, wall sculpture, and beauty of parklike floor, like most other great canyons, it has no waterfalls in sight, and no appreciable floor spaces. The big river has just room enough to flow and roar obscurely, here and there groping its way as best it can, like a weary, murmuring, overladen traveler trying to escape from the tremendous, bewildering labyrinthic abyss, while its roar serves only to deepen the silence. Instead of being filled with air, the vast space between the walls is crowded with Nature's grandest buildings—a sublime city of them, painted in every color, and adorned with richly fretted cornice and battlement spire and tower in endless variety of style and architecture. Every architectural invention of man has been anticipated, and far more, in this grandest of God's terrestrial cities.

Perhaps the greatest feel for the total Canyon effect—of form, color, light, and mood—can be obtained from the writing of the first geologist to immerse himself in the Canyon, Clarence E. Dutton, a U.S. Army captain, who was the Powell Survey geologist and spent many years in the 1870's and 1880's studying the district.

It may seem strange to turn to a geologist for the feel of the Canyon, but he was its lover as well as its student. And he was gifted with a talent for writing which he indulged, with appropriate apology. As he explained:

> I have in many places departed from the severe ascetic style which has become conventional in scientific monographs. Perhaps no apology is called for. Under ordinary circumstances the ascetic discipline is necessary. Give the imagination an inch and it is apt to take an ell, and the fundamental requirement of scientific method—accuracy of statement—is imperiled. But in the Grand Canyon district there is no such danger. The stimulants which are demoralizing elsewhere are necessary here to exalt the mind sufficiently to comprehend the sublimity of the subjects. Their sublimity has in fact been hitherto underrated. Great as is the fame of the Grand Canyon of the Colorado, the half remains to be told.

In any event, I know of no better way of communicating the complex impact of the Canyon than by sharing the understanding and enthusiasm of Dutton as expressed in his *Tertiary History of the Grand Cañon District*, published over ninety years ago:

> Wherever we reach the Grand Canyon in the Kaibab it bursts upon the vision in a moment. Seldom is any warning given that we are near the brink. . . . If the approach is made at random, with no idea of reaching any particular point by a known route, the probabilities are that it is first seen from the rim of one of the vast amphitheaters which set back from the main chasm far into the mass of the plateau. . . . Of course there are degrees in the magnitude and power of the pictures presented, but the smallest and least powerful is tremendous and too great for comprehension. The scenery of the amphitheaters far surpasses in grandeur and nobility anything else of the kind in any other region, but it is mere byplay in comparison with the panorama displayed in the heart of the canyon. The supreme views are to be obtained at the extremities of the long promontories, which jut out between these recesses far into the gulf. . . .
>
> Reaching the extreme verge the [back] packs are cast off, and sitting upon the edge we contemplate the most sublime and awe-inspiring spectacle in the world.
>
> The Grand Canyon of the Colorado is a great innovation in modern ideas of scenery, and in our conceptions of the grandeur, beauty, and power of nature. As with all great innovations it is not to be comprehended in a day or a week, nor even in a month. It must be dwelt upon and studied, and the study must comprise the slow acquisition of the meaning and spirit of that marvelous scenery which characterizes the Plateau Country, and of which the great chasm is the superlative manifestation. The study and slow mastery of the influences of that class of scenery and its full appreciation is a special culture, requiring time, patience, and long familiarity for its consummation. The lover of nature, whose perceptions have been trained in the Alps, in Italy, Germany, or New England, in the Appalachians or Cordilleras, in Scotland or Colorado, would enter this strange region with a shock, and dwell there for a time with a

sense of oppression, and perhaps with horror. Whatsoever things he had learned to regard as beautiful and noble he would seldom or never see, and whatsoever he might see would appear to him as anything but beautiful and noble. Whatsoever might be bold and striking would at first seem only grotesque. The colors would be the very ones he had learned to shun as tawdry and bizarre. The tones and shades, modest and tender, subdued yet rich, in which his fancy had always taken special delight, would be the ones that are conspicuously absent. But time would bring a gradual change. Someday he would suddenly become conscious that outlines, which at first seemed harsh and trivial, have grace and meaning; that forms which seemed grotesque are full of dignity; that magnitudes which had added enormity to coarseness have become replete with strength and even majesty; that colors which had been esteemed unrefined, immodest, and glaring, are as expressive, tender, changeful, and capacious of effects as any others. Great innovations, whether in art or literature, in science or in nature, seldom take the world by storm. They must be understood before they can be estimated, and must be cultivated before they can be understood.

It is so with the Grand Canyon. The observer who visits its commanding points with the expectation of experiencing forthwith a rapturous exaltation, an ecstasy arising from the realization of a degree of grandeur and sublimity never felt before, is doomed to disappointment. Supposing him to be but little familiar with plateau scenery, he will be simply bewildered. Must he, therefore, pronounce it a failure, an overpraised thing? Must he entertain a just resentment toward those who may have raised his expectations too high? The answer is that subjects which disclose their full power, meaning, and beauty as soon as they are presented to the mind have very little of those qualities to disclose. Moreover, a visitor to the chasm or to any other famous scene must necessarily come there (for so is the human mind constituted) with a picture of it created by his own imagination. He reaches the spot, the conjured picture vanishes in an instant, and the place of it must be filled anew. Surely no imagination can construct out of its own material any picture having the remotest resemblance to the Grand Canyon. In truth, the first step in attempting a description is to beg the reader to dismiss from his mind, so far as practicable, any preconceived notion of it.

Those who have long and carefully studied the Grand Canyon of the Colorado do not hesitate for a moment to pronounce it by far the most sublime of all earthly spectacles. If its sublimity consisted only in its dimensions, it could be sufficiently set forth in a single sentence. It is more than two hundred miles long, from five to twelve miles wide, and from five thousand to six thousand feet deep. There are in the world valleys which are longer and a few which are deeper. There are valleys flanked by summits loftier than the palisades of the Kaibab. Still the Grand Canyon is the sublimest thing on earth. It is so not alone by virtue of its magnitudes, but by virtue of the whole—its *ensemble*.

The common notion of a canyon is that of a deep, narrow gash in the earth, with nearly vertical walls, like a great and neatly cut trench. There are hundreds of chasms in the Plateau Country which answer very well to this notion. Many of them are sunk to frightful depths and are fifty to a hundred miles in length. Some are exceedingly narrow, as the canyons of the forks of the Virgen, where the overhanging walls shut out the sky. Some are intricately sculptured and illuminated with brilliant colors; others are picturesque by reason of their bold and striking sculpture. A few of them are most solemn and impressive by reason of their profundity and the majesty of their walls. But, as a rule, the common canyons are neither grand nor even attractive. Upon first acquaintance they are curious and awaken interest as a new sensation, but they soon grow tiresome for want of diversity, and become at last mere bores. The impressions they produce are very transient, because of their great simplicity and the limited range of ideas they present. But there are some which are highly diversified, presenting many attractive features. These seldom grow stale or wearisome, and their presence is generally greeted with pleasure.

It is perhaps in some respects unfortunate that the stupendous pathway of the Colorado River through the Kaibabs was ever called a canyon, for the name identifies it with the baser conception. But the name presents as wide a range of signification as the word house. The log cabin of the rancher, the painted and vine-clad cottage of the mechanic, the home of the millionaire, the places where parliaments assemble, and the grandest temples of worship, are all houses. Yet the contrast between St. Mark's and the rude dwelling of the frontiersman is not greater than that between the chasm of the Colorado and the trenches in the rocks which answer to the ordinary conception of a canyon. And as a great cathedral is an immense development of the rudimentary idea involved in the four walls and roof of a cabin, so is the chasm an expansion of the simple type of drainage channels peculiar to the Plateau Country. To the conception of its vast proportions must be added some notion of its intricate plan, the nobility of its architecture, its colossal buttes, its wealth of ornamentation, the splendor of its colors, and its wonderful atmosphere. All of these attributes combine with infinite complexity to produce a whole which at first bewilders and at length overpowers.

. . . both walls [of the Canyon] are recessed by wide amphitheaters, setting far back into the platform of the country, and the promontories are comparatively narrow strips between them. A . . . statement of the general width would be from eleven to twelve miles. This must dispose at once of the idea that the chasm is a narrow gorge of immense depth and simple form. It is somewhat unfortunate that there is a prevalent idea that in some way an essential part of the grandeur of the Grand Canyon is the narrowness of its defiles. Much color has been given to this notion by the first illustrations of the Canyon from the pencil of Egloffstein in the celebrated report of Lieutenant Ives. Never was a great subject more artistically misrepresented or more charmingly belittled. Nowhere in the Kaibab section is any such extreme narrowness observable, and even in the Uinkaret section the width of the great inner gorge is a little greater than the depth. In truth, a little reflection will show that such a character would be inconsistent with the highest and strongest effects. For it is obvious that some notable width is necessary to enable the eye to see the full extent of the walls. In a chasm one mile deep, and only a thousand feet wide, this would be quite impossible. If we compare the Marble Canyon or the gorge at the Toroweap with wider sections it will at once be seen that the wider ones are much stronger. If we compare one of the longer alcoves having a width of three or four miles with the view across the main chasm the advantage will be overwhelmingly with the latter. It is evident that for the display of wall surface of given dimensions a certain amount of distance is necessary. We may be too near or too far for the right appreciation of its magnitude and proportions. The distance must bear some ratio to the magnitude. But at what precise limit this distance must in the present case be fixed is not easy to determine. It can hardly be doubted that if the Canyon were materially narrower it would suffer a loss of grandeur and effect.

The space under immediate view from our standpoint, fifty miles long and ten to twelve wide, is thronged with a great multitude of objects so vast in size, so bold yet majestic in form, so infinite in their details, that as the truth gradually reveals itself to the perceptions it arouses the strongest emotions. Unquestionably the great, the overruling feature is the wall on the opposite side of the gulf. Can mortal fancy create a picture of a mural front a mile in height, seven to ten miles distant, and receding into space indefinitely in either direction? As the mind strives to realize its proportions its spirit is broken and its imagination completely crushed. If the wall were simple in its character, if it were only blank and sheer, some rest might be found in contemplating it; but it is full of diversity and eloquent with grand suggestions. It is deeply recessed by alcoves and amphitheaters receding far into the plateau beyond, and usually disclosing only the portals by which they open into the main chasm. Between them the promontories jut out, ending in magnificent gables with sharp-mitered angles. Thus the wall rambles in and out, turning numberless corners. Many of the angles are acute, and descend as sharp spurs like the forward edge of a plowshare. Only those alcoves which are directly opposite to us can be seen in their full length and depth. Yet so excessive, nay so prodigious, is the effect of foreshortening, that it is impossible to realize their full extensions. . . . At many points the profile of the façade is thrown into view by the change of trend, and its complex character is fully revealed. Like that of the Vermilion Cliffs, it is a series of many ledges and slopes, like a molded plinth, in which every stratum is disclosed as a line or a course of masonry. The Red Wall limestone is the most conspicuous member, presenting its vertical face [five hundred to five hundred fifty feet high], and everywhere unbroken. The thinner beds more often appear in the slopes as a succession of ledges projecting through the scanty talus which never conceals them.

Numerous detached masses are also seen flanking the ends of the long promontories. These buttes are of gigantic proportions, and yet so overwhelming is the effect of the wall against which they are projected that they seem insignificant in mass, and the observer is often deluded by them, failing to perceive that they are really detached from the wall and perhaps separated from it by an interval of a mile or two.

At the foot of this palisade is a platform through which meanders the inner gorge, in whose dark and somber depths flows the river. Only in one place can the water surface be seen. In its windings the abyss which holds it extends for a short distance toward us and the line of vision enters the gorge lengthwise. Above and below this short reach the gorge swings its course in other directions and reveals only a dark, narrow opening, while its nearer wall hides its depths. This inner chasm is one thousand to [fifteen hundred] feet deep. Its upper two hundred feet is a vertical ledge of sandstone of a dark, rich, brownish color. Beneath it lies the granite of a dark iron-gray shade, verging toward black, and lending a gloomy aspect to the lowest deeps. Perhaps a half mile of the river is disclosed. A pale, dirty red, without glimmer or sheen, a motionless surface, a small featureless spot, inclosed in the dark shade of the granite, is all of it that is here visible. Yet we know it is a large river, a hundred and fifty yards wide, with a headlong torrent foaming and plunging over rocky rapids.

A little, and only a little, less impressive than the great wall across the chasm are the buttes upon this side. And such buttes! All others in the west, saving only the peerless temples of the Virgen, are mere trifles in comparison with those of the Grand Canyon. In nobility of form, beauty of decoration, and splendor of color, the temples of the Virgen must, on the whole, be awarded the palm; but those of the Grand Canyon, while barely inferior to them in those respects, surpass them in magnitude and fully equal them in majesty. But while the valley of the Virgen presents a few of these superlative creations, the Grand Canyon presents them by dozens. In this relation the comparison would be analogous to one between a fine cathedral town and a metropolis like London or Paris. In truth, there is only a very limited ground of comparison between the two localities, for in style and effects their respective structures differ as decidedly as the works of any two well-developed and strongly contrasted styles of human architecture.

On either side of the promontory on which we stand is a side gorge sinking nearly four thousand feet below us. . . . The whole prospect, indeed, is filled with a great throng of similar objects, which, as much by their multitude as by their colossal size, confuse the senses; but these, on account of their proximity, may be most satisfactorily studied. The infinity of sharply defined detail is amazing. The eye is instantly caught and the attention firmly held by its systematic character. The parallelism of the lines of bedding is most forcibly displayed in all the windings of the façades, and these lines are crossed by the vertical scorings of numberless waterways. Here, too, are distinctly seen those details which constitute the peculiar style of decoration prevailing throughout all the buttes and amphitheaters of the Kaibab. The course of the walls is never for a moment straight, but extends as a series of cusps and re-entrant curves. Elsewhere the reverse is more frequently seen; the projections of the wall are rounded and are convex toward the front, while the re-entrant portions are cusplike recesses. . . .

As we contemplate these objects we find it quite impossible to realize their magnitude. Not only are we deceived, but we are conscious that we are deceived, and yet we cannot conquer the deception. We cannot long study our surroundings without becoming aware of an enormous disparity in the effects produced upon the senses by objects which are immediate and equivalent ones which are more remote. The depth of the gulf . . . cannot be realized. We crane over the brink, and about seven hundred feet below is a talus, which ends at the summit of the cross-bedded sandstone. We may see the bottom of the gorge, which is about thirty-eight hundred feet beneath us, and yet the talus seems at least halfway down. Looking across the side gorge the cross-bedded sandstone is seen as a mere band at the summit of the Cloister, forming but a very small portion of its vertical extent, and, whatever the reason may conclude, it is useless to attempt to persuade the imagination that the two edges of the sandstone lie in the same horizontal plane. The eastern Cloister is nearer than the western, its distance being about a mile and a half. It seems incredible that it can be so much as one third that distance. Its altitude is from thirty-five hundred to four thousand feet, but any attempt to estimate the altitude by means of visual impressions is felt at once to be hopeless. There is no stadium.

Dimensions mean nothing to the senses, and all that we are conscious of in this respect is a troubled sense of immensity. . . .

In all the vast space beneath and around us there is very little upon which the mind can linger restfully. It is completely filled with objects of gigantic size and amazing form, and as the mind wanders over them it is hopelessly bewildered and lost. It is useless to select special points of contemplation. The instant the attention lays hold of them it is drawn to something else, and if it seeks to recur to them it cannot find them. Everything is superlative, transcending the power of the intelligence to comprehend it. There is no central point or object around which the other elements are grouped and to which they are tributary. The grandest objects are merged in a congregation of others equally grand. Hundreds of these mighty structures, miles in length, and thousands of feet in height, rear their majestic heads out of the abyss, displaying their richly molded plinths and friezes, thrusting out their gables, wing walls, buttresses, and pilasters, and recessed with alcoves and panels. If any one of these stupendous creations had been planted upon the plains of central Europe it would have influenced modern art as profoundly as Fujiyama has influenced the decorative art of Japan. Yet here they are all swallowed up in the confusion of multitude. It is not alone the magnitude of the individual objects that makes this spectacle so portentous, but it is still more the extravagant profusion with which they are arrayed along the whole visible extent of the broad chasm.

The color effects are rich and wonderful. They are due to the inherent colors of the rocks, modified by the atmosphere. Like any other great series of strata in the Plateau Province, the Carboniferous has its own range of characteristic colors, which might serve to distinguish it even if we had no other criterion. The summit strata are pale gray, with a faint yellowish cast. Beneath them the cross-bedded sandstone appears, showing a mottled surface of pale pinkish hue. Underneath this member are nearly one thousand feet of the lower Aubrey sandstones, displaying an intensely brilliant red, which is somewhat masked by the talus shot down from the gray, cherty limestones at the summit. Beneath the lower Aubrey is the face of the Red Wall limestone. . . . It has a strong red tone, but a very peculiar one. Most of the red strata of the west have the brownish or vermilion tones, but these are rather purplish red, as if the pigment had been treated to a dash of blue. It is not quite certain that this may not arise in part from the intervention of the blue haze, and probably it is rendered more conspicuous by this cause; but, on the whole, the purplish cast seems to be inherent. This is the dominant color mass of the Canyon, for the expanse of rock surface displayed is more than half in the Red Wall group. It is less brilliant than the fiery red of the Aubrey sandstones, but is still quite strong and rich. Beneath are the deep browns of the lower Carboniferous. The dark iron-black of the hornblendic schists revealed in the lower gorge makes but little impression upon the boundless expanse of bright colors above.

The total effect of the entire color mass is bright and glowing. There is nothing gloomy or dark in the picture, except the opening of the inner gorge, which is too small a feature to influence materially the prevailing tone. Although the colors are bright when contrasted with normal landscapes, they are decidedly less intense than the flaming hues of the Trias or the dense, cloying colors of the Permian; nor have they the refinement of those revealed in the Eocene. The intense luster which gleams from the rocks of the Plateau Country is by no means lost here, but is merely subdued and kept under some restraint. It is toned down and softened without being deprived of its character. Enough of it is left to produce color effects not far below those that are yielded by the Jura-Trias.

But though the inherent colors are less intense than some others, yet under the quickening influence of the atmosphere they produce effects to which all others are far inferior. And here language fails and description becomes impossible. Not only are their qualities exceedingly subtle, but they have little counterpart in common experience. If such are presented elsewhere they are presented so feebly and obscurely that only the most discriminating and closest observers of nature ever seize them, and then so imperfectly that their ideas of them are vague and but half real. There are no concrete notions founded in experience upon which a conception of these color effects and optical delusions can be constructed and made intelligible. A perpetual glamour envelops the landscape. Things are not what they seem, and the perceptions cannot tell us what they are. It is not probable that these effects are different in kind in the Grand Canyon from what they are in other portions of the Plateau Country. But the difference in degree is immense, and being greatly magnified and intensified many characteristics become palpable which elsewhere elude the closest observation.

In truth, the tone and temper of the landscape are constantly varying, and the changes in its aspect are very great. It is never the same, even from day to day, or even from hour to hour. In the early morning its mood and subjective influences are usually calmer and more full of repose than at other times, but as the sun rises higher the whole scene is so changed that we cannot recall our first impressions. Every passing cloud, every change in the position of the sun, recasts the whole. At sunset the pageant closes amid splendors that seem more than earthly. The direction of the full sunlight, the massing of the shadows, the manner in which the side lights are thrown in from the clouds determine these modulations, and the sensitiveness of the picture to the slightest variations in these conditions is very wonderful.

The shadows thrown by the bold abrupt forms are exceedingly dark. It is almost impossible at the distance of a very few miles to distinguish even broad details in these shadows. They are like remnants of midnight unconquered by the blaze of noonday. The want of half tones and gradations in the light and shade, which has already been noted in the Vermilion Cliffs, is apparent here, and is far more conspicuous. Our thoughts in this connection may suggest to us a still more extreme case of a similar phenomenon presented by the half-illuminated moon when viewed through a large telescope. The portions which catch the sunlight shine with great luster, but the shadows of mountains and cliffs are black and impenetrable. But there is one feature in the Canyon which is certainly extraordinary. It is the appearance of the atmosphere against the background of shadow. It has a metallic luster which must be seen to be appreciated. The great wall across the chasm presents at noonday, under a cloudless sky, a singularly weird and unearthly aspect. The color is for the most part gone. In place of it comes this metallic glare of the haze. The southern wall is never so poorly lighted as at noon. Since its face consists of a series of promontories projecting toward the north, these projections catch the sunlight on their eastern sides in the forenoon, and upon their western sides in the afternoon; but near meridian the rays fall upon a few points only, and even upon these with very great obliquity. Thus at the hours of greatest general illumination the wall is most obscure and the abnormal effects are then presented most forcibly. They give rise to strange delusions. The rocks then look nearly black, or very dark gray, and covered with feebly shining spots. The haze is strongly luminous, and so dense as to obscure the details already enfeebled by shade as if a leaden or mercurial vapor intervened. The shadows antagonize the perspective, and everything seems awry. The lines of stratification, dimly seen in one place and wholly effaced in another, are strangely belied, and the strata are given apparent attitudes which are sometimes grotesque and sometimes impossible.

Those who are familiar with western scenery have, no doubt, been impressed with the peculiar character of its haze—or atmosphere, in the artistic sense of the word—and have noted its more prominent qualities. When the air is free from common smoke it has a pale blue color which is quite unlike the neutral gray of the east. It is always apparently more dense when we look toward the sun than when we look away from it, and this difference in the two directions, respectively, is at a maximum near sunrise and sunset. This property is universal, but its peculiarities in the Plateau Country become conspicuous when the strong, rich colors of the rocks are seen through it. The very air is then visible. We see it, palpably, as a tenuous fluid, and the rocks beyond it do not appear to be colored blue as they do in other regions, but reveal themselves clothed in colors of their own. The Grand Canyon is ever full of this haze. It fills it to the brim. Its apparent density, as elsewhere, is varied according to the direction in which it is viewed and the position of the sun; but it seems also to be denser and more concentrated than elsewhere. This is really a delusion arising from the fact that the enormous magnitude of the chasm and of its component masses dwarfs the distances; we are really looking through miles of atmosphere under the impression that they are only so many furlongs. This apparent concentration of haze, however, greatly intensifies all the beautiful or mysterious optical defects which are dependent upon the intervention of the atmosphere.

Whenever the brink of the chasm is reached the chances are that the sun is high and these abnormal effects in full force. The Canyon is asleep. Or it is under a spell of enchantment which gives its bewildering mazes an aspect still more bewildering. Throughout the long summer forenoon the charm which binds it grows in potency. At midday the clouds begin to gather, first in fleecy flecks, then in cumuli, and throw their shadows into the gulf. At once the scene changes. The slumber of the chasm is disturbed. The temples and cloisters seem to raise themselves half awake to greet the passing shadow. Their wilted, drooping, flattened faces expand into relief. The long promontories reach out from the distant wall as if to catch a moment's refreshment from the shade. The colors begin to glow; the haze loses its opaque density and becomes more tenuous. The shadows pass, and the chasm relapses into its dull sleep again. Thus through the midday hours it lies in fitful slumber, overcome by the blinding glare and withering heat, yet responsive to every fluctuation of light and shadow like a delicate organism.

As the sun moves far into the west the scene again changes, slowly and imperceptibly at first, but afterward more rapidly. In the hot summer afternoons the sky is full of cloud play. . . . The banks of snowy clouds pour a flood of light sidewise into the shadows and light up the gloom of the amphitheaters and alcoves, weakening the glow of the haze and rendering visible the details of the wall faces. At length, as the sun draws near the horizon, the great drama of the day begins.

Throughout the afternoon the prospect has been gradually growing clearer. The haze has relaxed its steely glare and has changed to a veil of transparent blue. Slowly the myriads of details have come out and the walls are flecked with lines of minute tracery, forming a diaper of light and shade. Stronger and sharper becomes the relief of each projection. The promontories come forth from the opposite wall. The sinuous lines of stratification, which once seemed meaningless, distorted, and even chaotic, now range themselves into a true perspective of graceful curves, threading the scallop edges of the strata. The colossal buttes expand in every dimension. Their long, narrow wings, which once were folded together and flattened against each other, open out, disclosing between them vast alcoves illumined with Rembrandt lights tinged with the pale refined blue of the ever-present haze. A thousand forms, hitherto unseen or obscure, start up within the abyss, and stand forth in strength and animation. All things seem to grow in beauty, power, and dimensions. What was grand before has become majestic, the majestic becomes sublime, and, ever expanding and developing, the sublime passes beyond the reach of our faculties and becomes transcendent. The colors have come back. Inherently rich and strong, though not superlative under ordinary lights, they now begin to display an adventitious brilliancy. The western sky is all aflame. The scattered banks of cloud and wavy cirrus have caught the waning splendor, and shine with orange and crimson. Broad slant beams of yellow light, shot through the glory rifts, fall on turret and tower, on pinnacled crest and winding ledge, suffusing them with a radiance less fulsome, but akin to that which flames in the western clouds. The summit band is brilliant yellow; the next below is pale rose. But the grand expanse within is a deep, luminous, resplendent red. The climax has now come. The blaze of sunlight poured over an illimitable surface of glowing red is flung back into the gulf, and, commingling with the blue haze, turns it into a sea of purple of most imperial hue—so rich, so strong, so pure that it makes the heart ache and the throat tighten. However vast the magnitudes, however majestic the forms, or sumptuous the decoration, it is in these kingly colors that the highest glory of the Grand Canyon is revealed.

At length the sun sinks and the colors cease to burn. The abyss lapses back into repose. But its glory mounts upward and diffuses itself in the sky above. Long streamers of rosy light, rayed out from the west, cross the firmament and converge again in the east, ending in a pale rosy arch, which rises like a low aurora just above the eastern horizon. Below it is the dead gray shadow of the world. Higher and higher climbs the arch, followed by the darkening pall of gray, and as it ascends, it fades and disappears, leaving no color except the afterglow of the western clouds and the lusterless red of the chasm below. Within the abyss the darkness gathers. Gradually the shades deepen and ascend, hiding the opposite wall and enveloping the great temples. For a few moments the summits of these majestic piles seem to float upon a sea of blackness, then vanish in the darkness, and, wrapped in the impenetrable mantle of the night, they await the glory of the coming dawn.

Sunrise

Nature is an incredible complexity of changing light, color, form, and mood—from season to season, day to day, within any day, and even from moment to moment. Nowhere has nature expressed this infinite variability as powerfully as at the Canyon.

The Canyon needs no special moods of nature to provide a fascinating variety of scenic splendor. Except for the middle of the day, when the light tends to obscure both form and color, the westward procession of the sun provides a constant novelty of view, as if the Canyon were being continuously re-created.

C. A. Higgins, a nineteenth-century visitor to the Canyon, described its changing aspects:

. . . the panorama is the real overmastering charm. It is never twice the same. Although you think you have spelt out every temple and peak and escarpment, as the angle of sunlight changes there begins a ghostly advance of colossal forms from the farther side, and what you had taken to be the ultimate wall is seen to be made up of still other isolated sculptures, revealed now for the first time by silhouetting shadows. The scene incessantly changes, flushing and fading, advancing into crystalline clearness, retiring into slumbrous haze.

The joyous pageant of sunrise at the Canyon is unveiled from second to second, light leaping from peak to peak, transforming the world from darkness to the exultation of colorful, shining cliffs and temples.

The first flush of sunrise at Hopi Point, with the red-orange-gold succession of Kaibab limestone gleaming above the vivid reds that blaze out of the purplish depths, is a thrilling enough experience. But when flaming storm clouds enrich the sunrise scene and isolated peaks and cliffs blaze out against the darkness, the viewer is entranced.

The West Rim

The perspectives of the Canyon are best seen from the rims, each of which has its own special beauties: the West Rim (of the South Rim) provides the most majestic array of temples, the East Rim (of the South Rim) offers the most colorful panoramas, and the North Rim presents the most powerful temples. The grandeur of the Canyon is inescapable at all the rims and from any point on any rim.

Almost all the major Canyon temples (the buttes that are most impressive in size and form) have been eroded from the North Rim, but these are normally best viewed from the South Rim; unless they are seen from a distance, they lose much of their awesome aspect and complex configuration. The Colorado River is most dramatic from the closer South Rim; the North Rim's stunningly carved Bright Angel Canyon may be viewed to advantage from the South Rim only; and the South Rim light presents the colors of the Canyon more vividly.

For maximum enjoyment, viewing the Canyon from the rims involves both skill and prudence. The most thrilling views are often seen from the extreme edge of a precipitous cliff—every inch closer to the edge adds immeasurably to the sense of depth.

For some viewers, fear predominates. As Mrs. John T. Varmer wrote in 1892, "I have never witnessed anything like this. It scares me to even try to look down into it. My God, I am afraid the whole country will fall into this great hole in the ground."

Every such approach should be made with great caution. Even James Wesley Powell, the audacious pioneer explorer of the Colorado River, respected the canyon brink:

> After a good drink we walk out to the brink of the canyon and look down to the water below. I can do this now, but it has taken several years of mountain climbing to cool my nerves so that I can sit with my feet over the edge and calmly look down a precipice two thousand feet. And yet I cannot look on and see another do the same. I must either bid him come away or turn my head.

And perhaps no one but the dauntless, one-armed Powell would ever find himself in the predicament he calmly described:

> High above the river we can walk along on the top of the granite, which is broken off at the edge and set with crags and pinnacles, so that it is very difficult to get a view of the river at all. In my eagerness to reach a point where I can see the roaring fall below, I go too far on the wall, and can neither advance nor retreat. I stand with one foot on a little projecting rock and cling with my hand fixed in a little crevice. Finding I am caught here, suspended four hundred feet above the river, into which I must fall if my footing fails, I call for help. The men come and pass me a line, but I cannot let go of the rock long enough to take hold of it. Then they bring two or three of the largest oars. All this takes time which seems very precious to me; but at last they arrive. The blade of one of the oars is pushed into a little crevice in the rock beyond me in such a manner that they can hold me pressed against the wall. Then another is fixed in such a way that I can step on it; and thus I am extricated.

Some of the Canyon's viewers shrink from the Canyon in fear and others find its views uninspiring. One of the early (1858) explorers of the Canyon, Lieutenant Joseph C. Ives, noted:

> Ours has been the first, and doubtless will be the last party of whites to visit this profitless locality. It seems intended by nature that the Colorado River, along the greater portion of its lonely and majestic way, shall be forever unvisited and undisturbed.

And even modern enthusiasts of the Canyon may find it difficult to appreciate its beauty without prolonged acquaintance. As Joseph Wood Krutch wrote:

> At first glance . . . it stuns the eye but cannot really hold the attention. . . . We cannot realize that the tremendous masses and curiously shaped buttes . . . are the grandiose objects they are. . . . Because we cannot relate to it, we remain outside, very much as we remain outside of a picture. . . . To get into the picture . . . is not easy to do in a short time.

Fortunately for me, as for many other viewers, my first vision of the Canyon inspired an instant and overwhelming response—I was "inside" the Canyon with total absorption.

Harrison Gray Otis, one of the Canyon's early visitors, described his reaction with appropriate extravagance:

> Suddenly the awful majesty of the Grand Canyon is revealed to his startled vision. There before him lies the mighty red rift in the earth, the most stupendous gorge within the knowledge of man. The mind is spellbound by the spectacle; the voice is silent; the heart is subdued; the soul turns in profound reverence to the Almighty, whose handiwork is here seen on a colossal scale. No matter how many descriptions of the Grand Canyon may have been previously read by him who sees it for the first time, its profound depths, its colossal heights, its myriad and matchless colors, its brilliant hues, its striking lights and shades, its mighty sinuosities, and its altogether grand ensemble will fill the beholder with a mingled sense of awe, wonder, admiration, and reverence.

The West Rim (of the South Rim) offers the most intricate Canyon perspectives. The eye plunges steeply down the near cliffs, across the broad Tonto Plateau, into the forbidding sheer walls of the tough Granite Gorge, down to the rushing Colorado River below, and then up the steep and terraced buttes and temples to the rugged layers of the seemingly endless North Rim wall across the chasm.

Only from the West Rim may one see the multitude of magnificent temples surrounding Bright Angel Canyon, infinitely varied patterns of form, color, light, and shadow. The name was bestowed by Powell on the creek by which it was carved:

> The Colorado is never a clear stream, but for the past three or four days it has been raining much of the time, and the floods poured over the walls have brought down great quantities of mud, making it exceedingly turbid now. The little affluent which we have discovered here is a clear, beautiful creek, or river, as it would be termed in this western country, where streams are not abundant. We have named one stream, away above, in honor of the great chief of the "Bad Angels," and as this is in beautiful contrast to that, we conclude to name it "Bright Angel."

Flanked by innumerable grand forms, among which are Isis and Buddha to the west and Brahma and Zoroaster to the east, Bright Angel Canyon composes its most interesting panorama from Mather Point and reveals its intricacies most impressively from Yavapai Point.

Stretching for about ten miles from the junction of the east and south entrance roads, the West

Rim presents almost a crowd of viewpoints. To the casual observer they all seem pretty much the same—a confusing multitude of overwhelming and colorful forms. But each viewpoint has its own virtues, if only one is sufficiently awake. As Thoreau said, "To be awake is to be alive. I have never met a man who was quite awake. How could I have looked him in the face?"

Mather not only has the most harmoniously composed panorama of Bright Angel Canyon temples, it also offers a diversity of gorgeous sunrise scenes. The succession of projecting walls reflects the dazzling rays of the rising sun, each wall with its own distinctive glow. Some of the most fantastically carved canyon forms may be seen at Mather just below the rim—especially beautiful at sunrise.

Yavapai displays the finest portraits of the West Rim temples—the confusing canyon forms seem to arrange themselves here in individual poses for the viewer's delight. The Colorado River is dramatically exposed at the base of the Granite Gorge, here over one thousand feet deep, which rises massive, dark, and rugged.

Pima presents the broadest West Rim panorama, with seemingly endless views of buttes and temples. Many beautiful views of the Colorado River lie far below, displayed with greatest impact at Granite Rapids below Monument Creek, just east of the point.

My favorite West Rim viewpoint is at Hopi. The panorama is not quite as broad as at Pima; the temples are not as individually posed as at Yavapai, nor as classically arranged as at Mather. But sunrise at Hopi is a fabulous vision of form and color, and sunset at Hopi is, to me, the most moving of all canyon scenes.

The East Rim

The East Rim is a land of sweeping vistas and enchanting color. The fantastic array of Bright Angel temples no longer dominates the scene, but forms the background for some of its broad panoramas. The great canyon walls and temples still overwhelm the viewer, but the narrow, formidable Granite Gorge is here seen only from a distance; in its place is a broad valley formed by the mighty Colorado River here meandering in softer, tilted-rock formations.

These tilted rocks—the Grand Canyon Series, just below the horizontal formations that top the Canyon, only fragments of which are visible from the West Rim—are here laid bare, displaying the most brilliant canyon colors, predominantly red. Viewed from Lipan Point, especially, the crimson hues are unusually vivid.

The irregular appearance of much of the East Rim was described by an early canyon visitor, R. B. Stanton:

> This first section of the Grand Canyon, from the Little Colorado to the beginning of the Granite Gorge, some eighteen miles in distance, is one of great interest. The whole section

seems to have been upturned, tumbled over, and mixed in every imaginable shape, some of the oldest and newest formations standing side by side, showing most gorgeous coloring of mineralized matter, from dark purple and green to bright red and yellow. The river runs through quite a wide valley, with bottom lands and groves of mesquite. The top walls of the Canyon are miles and miles apart, and hills and knobs rise between the river and the walls beyond, these being separated by deep washes and gulches running in every direction.

Extending for over twenty miles east of the junction of the east and south entrance roads, the East Rim is more varied in outlook than the West Rim. Its many viewpoints are more widely spaced, with at least four deserved favorites—Grandview, Moran, Lipan, and Desert View.

Of all canyon panoramas, Grandview is the most intimate—the awesome dimensions of the Canyon seem reduced to almost comprehensible proportions, with the western and eastern sections presented in so balanced a perspective that it is hardly surprising that this viewpoint was the site of the first tourist hotel.

Moran, named for the pioneer western painter Thomas Moran, has much of the Grandview aspect, but it also provides some beautiful views of the Colorado River. Brilliant red color is displayed in the steep cliffs rising dramatically above the Colorado (directly below the viewer who finds a vantage point on a ledge below the rim) and above the sloping canyon valley through which the Colorado winds its way in the eastern distance.

There is along its length, an extensive, if undistinguished, ponderosa pine forest that stops just short of the South Rim and an intriguing display of fir trees decorates shaded slopes below the rim. Weirdly beautiful piñon pines and junipers form an integral part of the landscape, reaching out with contorted branches toward light and freedom. My favorite South Rim tree is a juniper at Moran, just below the top, tenaciously gripping the rocky soil and thrusting its arms to the sky.

Lipan Point, to me, presents more different kinds of fantastic beauty than any other point in the Canyon. To the left is the classic, steep cliff view at its most spectacular, with a sharply profiled wall dominating a seemingly endless succession of similar walls stretching to the western horizon. Just below this range of cliffs, to the right, is the churning Colorado, knifing through the dark Granite Gorge, which rises from the ruddy earth. In the center, an intricately carved North Rim wall is enriched by the grand forms of Wotan's Throne and Vishnu Temple. Toward the right a fantasy of flaming rock enfolds the Colorado as it curves below the graceful temples of Venus and Apollo, united here in one grand image. And in the east, below the often golden Palisades of the Desert and above the deep red of Escalante Butte, winds a seemingly gentle Colorado.

Desert View, at the east end of the East Rim, offers a varied panorama to the west and an almost unlimited view across the Painted Desert to the east. The Colorado, here making its entrance into the Canyon, leaves the towering walls behind and flows beneath the often rosy purple of its grandly rising banks. One of the Canyon's visual treasures is the steep wall of the Palisades of the Desert at sunset, glowing in successive tones of deepening gold, orange, and red.

The North Rim

The cooler North Rim climate, which closes the snow-packed roads to visitors from early October to late May, also offers the visitor a delightful summer vacation.

The most majestic canyon temples, displayed so grandly for viewing from the South Rim, were all carved from the North Rim wall. The higher elevation here (about one thousand feet above the South Rim), the greater precipitation (almost twice as much), and the direction of creek drainage (toward the Canyon instead of away from it as at the South Rim) have combined to produce a more deeply eroded and intricately sculptured section of the Canyon, as well as more beautifully forested. The side canyons of the North Rim probe more deeply into its wall, its points project farther into the Canyon, its cliff silhouette is more rugged, and the Colorado River is more distant from the rim, while the great temples, closer to the viewer, are more intimately and more powerfully displayed.

The traveler from the South Rim (about ten miles by air and two hundred and ten miles by road), journeying through the ponderosa-piñon pine-juniper South Rim forest and the colorful but barren Painted Desert, finds the lovely North Rim wilderness a refreshment to a somewhat parched soul. Its spruces, firs, and pines, not as majestic as the big trees of the Sierra Nevada and not monotonous like much of the Rocky Mountain lodgepole pine forest, are splendidly displayed in open, soaring variety of form, texture, and shades of cooling green.

The special glory of this coniferous forest, however, is the profusion of aspens, yellow-green in the spring and gold-sprinkled with orange and red—in the fall.

The Canyon itself, here as at the South Rim, is an overwhelming experience. The greater proximity to the major temples, however, has its disadvantages—the greatest forms are too close to be seen as a complex array of temples crowning a sweeping foreground of buttes. Even the individual temples may lose much of their beauty when seen too closely. But there is a feeling of intimacy with them, an intense involvement with the structure, texture, color, and light, which is often overpowering. As Dutton explains it:

> The simplicity of the work, its symmetry, the definiteness of profile, the sustained character, arouse the mind at once, and the magnitude of it can be appreciated the more fully because the attention is not distracted by an endless number of objects, all of which are about equally impressive.

In addition, one may discover unsuspected beauty in the temples familiar from South Rim viewing. Wotan's Throne is a fascinating sight from Cape Royal. From the South Rim it is seen as a squarish block complementing the grace of Vishnu Temple with its imposing mass. Viewed from Cape Royal it is a graceful curve of shining cliff, with many sections of special grandeur.

Point Sublime, at the end of a seventeen-mile-long primitive road from near the north entrance, offers the broadest canyon panorama as well as the closest North Rim view of the Colorado River and a multitude of buttes. Dutton noted that it:

> . . . is on the whole the most commanding [view] . . . though there are several others which might be regarded as very nearly equal to it, or as even more imposing in some respects. . . . The length of Canyon revealed clearly and in detail . . . is about twenty-five miles in each direction. Toward the northwest the vista terminates behind the projecting mass of Powell's Plateau. But again to the westward may be seen the crests of the upper walls . . . finally disappearing in the haze about seventy-five miles away.

Bright Angel Point, the destination of all North Rim Lodge visitors, displays the familiar temples that surround Bright Angel Canyon with greater bulk but less majesty than the South Rim view. The side canyons carved around the point, however, are deeply indented, steep, and beautifully carved. The walk to the point close to the Kaibab limestone (more boldly and cleanly carved than at the South Rim), with the soaring piñon pines thrusting out of the Kaibab rock, offers another intimate canyon beauty.

Point Imperial, the highest spot on the canyon rims (8,801 feet), presents an impressive array of buttes, here seen primarily as ridges, displaying the depth of canyon carving to excellent effect. The scene as a whole is picturesque, but what captures the imagination most intensely is the imperial form of Mount Hayden, a classic spire thrusting toward the sky.

My favorite North Rim viewpoint is at Cape Royal. Dutton described his first view in his usual engaging manner:

> . . . we at length reach the end of a promontory, from which we behold a panorama of the central chasm rivaling in grandeur that of Point Sublime. A part of it, however, is obscured by a vast cloister butte in front of the cape and in close proximity to us. But though it hides what lies beyond, it is in itself so imposing that it compensates the loss. To the south and west the vista of the Grand Canyon stretches away in the fullest measure of its sublimity. The congregation of wonderful structures, countless and vast, the profound lateral chasms, the still lower but unseen depths of the central abyss that holds the river, and the overwhelming palisade of the southern wall, are much the same in their general effects as at Point Sublime; but the kaleidoscope is turned and the arrangement differs. We named this place Cape Royal.

What thrills me most at Cape Royal, however, is the intimate and powerful view of the Canyon's great temples. Vishnu Temple (considered by Dutton the grandest of all canyon forms) and Wotan's Throne, unaided by supporting forms, step forward in steep and solitary majesty.

Formations and Forms

Sustaining the aesthetic wonders of the Canyon is its geological display. The American West, in general, is one enormous geology laboratory. Yosemite displays the results of glacial ice carving igneous rock; Zion exhibits the cutting power of a seemingly innocuous river, and at Yellowstone one may watch the surface of the earth being reshaped by its inner heat. But the greatest single laboratory is the Grand Canyon. Professor Ralph Tarr noted long ago, "Nowhere in all the world can the geologist obtain in a single glance such an impressive lesson in geology."

The series of canyons that constitute the Grand Canyon were graphically described by Powell:

> The Grand Canyon of the Colorado is a canyon composed of many canyons. It is a composite of thousands, of tens of thousands, of gorges. In like manner, each wall of the canyon is a composite structure, a wall composed of many walls, but never a repetition. Every one of these almost innumerable gorges is a world of beauty in itself. In the Grand Canyon there are thousands of gorges like that below Niagara Falls, and there are a thousand Yosemites. Yet all these canyons unite to form one grand canyon, the most sublime spectacle on the earth.

Viewed from top to bottom, the canyon wall is mainly an alternation of steep and sloping cliffs, beginning with the craggy Kaibab limestone that falls away abruptly almost beneath our feet, and ending, nearly a mile below, with the narrow Granite Gorge. In Powell's words:

> The escarpments formed by the cut edges of the rock are often vertical, sometimes terraced, and in some places the trends of the terraces are sloping. In these quiet curves vast amphitheaters are formed, now in vertical rocks, now in steps.

Each of the Great Canyon formations, usually hundreds of feet in height, is a remarkably regular layer of rock, quite homogeneous in composition and recording a separate era of earth history. The youngest is the Kaibab limestone at the top, about two hundred and fifty million years old, and the oldest is the Vishnu schist of the Granite Gorge at the bottom, about two billion years old.

The upper canyon formations, about three to four thousand feet of horizontal cliffs and ledges, spread from one end of the Canyon to the other and are repeated on the opposite walls of the Canyon, without substantial change in composition or order. This regularity, when combined with the intricacy of erosional carving, is the geological foundation of the beauty of the Canyon's forms and vistas. Dutton noted:

> The strata of each and every age were remarkably uniform over very large areas, and were deposited very nearly horizontally. Very analogous is the constancy of lithological characters.

As we trace the individual beds from place to place, we find their composition to be as persistent as their thickness. The sandstone of a given horizon is always and everywhere a sandstone, the limestone a limestone, the shale a shale. Even the minuter structure of the beds is similarly maintained and features which are almost abnormal are equally constant. . . .

Another consideration is as follows: as we pass vertically from one formation to another in the geological series, we observe the same diversity of lithological characters as is found in other regions.

Thus it will be noted that while the strata are remarkably homogeneous in their horizontal extensions, they are very heterogeneous in vertical range. And this heterogeneity is found not only in the chemical constituents, but also in the texture and in the mechanical properties of hardness, compactness, and solubility. This consideration is an important one, since upon it depends the result which is obtained by the attack of the eroding elements—the architecture of the cliffs and profiles.

Moreover, each formation has its own special beauty. Each steep cliff differs in form and texture from every other. The Kaibab limestone, craggily eroded, is fantastically decorated with weird forms. The next sheer cliff, the Coconino sandstone (below the Toroweap limestone), is a massive, precipitous scarp which highlights the Canyon near the top in all directions. The Redwall limestone (below the Supai steps) is a series of softly rounded curving amphitheaters, smoothly perpendicular as if carved by water. And the Vishnu schist of the dark Granite Gorge is dramatically rugged.

Each sloping cliff, too, has its own special attraction. The shady slopes of the Toroweap limestone are decorated with fir trees in many places. The Hermit shale (just above the Supai shale-sandstone) usually has a smooth sheen. The Supai displays an irregular series of small steps, alternately steep and sloping. And the Bright Angel shale (below the Red Wall limestone) gently slopes into a broad (Tonto) plateau which, from the West Rim, sets the stage for the great temples above it as well as for the Granite Gorge below.

The varieties of formation would be fascinating enough if they were all of one color. (The creamy Kaibab limestone, by itself, is a dazzling reflector of the bright gleam of sunrise and the deep glow of sunset.) But their basic effect stems from the rainbow hues which transform them —above all, the crimson glow that often floods the canyon chasm. At times, the Canyon soars from forbidding black to blazing red and finally to gold. The poet Joaquin Miller said:

> Color is king here. Take the grandest, sublimest thing the world has ever seen, fashion it as if the master minds "from the beginning" had wrought here, paint it as only the masters of old could paint, and you have El Grande Cañon del Colorado.

The unique harmony of canyon form and color was celebrated by the noted editor William Allen White:

> There is a lift and mass about these walls that fills the soul with unutterable things. Out between the diverging walls, if the time be early afternoon, the sun if plying his paintbrush on the peaks and hills below, while up Bright Angel Creek the blue shadows seem to be smudged

into the canvas in a rough, crass silhouette, as though God's elementary drawing class had been put in charge of the lines and angles. But the color—the great kaleidoscope of color that is streaked and splashed through this petrified silence, the symphony of the blues and browns and grays and yellows and pinks and reds, with the faint green tints of the scant vegetation of the place—the color is the work of old journeymen angels, who know what delights men's souls. . . . The details of the canyon—its bits of composition—are marvelous in this, they tally so perfectly with man's idea of art in the arrangement of the lines, the balancing of form, and the discipline of color.

The universe of variegated forms is described by Dutton with his usual felicity:

We look across the Grand Canyon to the country beyond. Between us and the opposite wall is an interval of twelve miles, thronged with those magnificent masses and intricate details which characterize the Kaibab division. A plexus of drainage channels heading all around the base of the upper encircling walls unite in a short trunk channel which enters the Colorado. Each branch and filament has cut a lateral chasm of immense depth, and between the gorges rise the residual masses, in the form of buttes. Some of these are gorgeous pagodas, sculptured in the usual fashion, and ending in sharp finials at the summit. Others are the cloister buttes with wing walls and gables, panels and alcoves. All are quarried out upon a superlative scale of magnitude, and every one of them is a marvel. The great number and intricacy of these objects confuse the senses and do not permit the eye to rest. The mind wanders incessantly from one to another, and cannot master the multitude of things crowded at once upon its attention. There are scores of these structures, any one of which, if it could be placed by itself upon some distant plain, would be regarded as one of the great wonders of the world. Yet here they crowd each other, and no one of them predominates sufficiently to form a central point in the picture. Still, the power and grandeur is quite beyond description.

The carving of the Canyon and its tributary canyons required a unique combination of circumstances, among which the primary factors were a powerful river, rising land, and a dry country. This spectacular phenomenon is an elaborate demonstration of the simple insight of Thoreau's: "The finest workers in stone are not copper or steel, but the gentle touches of air and water working at their leisure with a liberal allowance of time."

To understand the process in its complexity, the reader may turn to Appendix A, where Clarence Dutton states his basic views and, in turn, quotes liberally from G. K. Gilbert's *Geology of the Henry Mountains.*

The Colorado River

The Colorado River is the most impressive rock-carving tool in the history of the earth —exposing the most illuminating single record of our planet's history. But it is also a festival of beauty, with myriad shapes, colors, and settings.

It may be an arrow, as it knifes its way into the Granite Gorge, as seen from Lipan; a stately bend at Pima; a graceful ribbon at Moran; a sinuous whip near Desert View, or a voluptuous curve at Lipan.

At times its color lives up to its red (Colorado) name, but it is now normally blue or green, because of the silt-removing operation of Glen Canyon dam—a happy accident of that tragic despoliation of beauty. In the west the Colorado displays its beauty beneath the massive Granite Gorge. In the east the Colorado's lovely blues and greens wind their graceful way through banks of red and purple.

The canyon rocks, through which the river flows, add their marvels to its splendors—with the stern, simple grandeur of the rugged Vishnu schist in the Granite Gorge, the lyric loveliness of gentler slopes enfolding the Colorado in the east, and the variety of canyon forms and patterns enriching every scene.

The sources of the Colorado, here often surrounded by flaming rock, lie in the cold heights of the Rocky Mountains, as noted by Powell:

> The Colorado River is formed by the junction of the Grand and Green.
>
> The Grand River has its source in the Rocky Mountains, five or six miles west of Long's Peak. A group of little alpine lakes, which receive their waters directly from perpetual snowbanks, discharge into a common reservoir known as Grand Lake, a beautiful sheet of water. Its quiet surface reflects towering cliffs and crags of granite on its eastern shore, and stately pines and firs stand on its western margin.
>
> The Green River heads near Fremont Peak, in the Wind River Range. This river, like the Grand, has its sources in alpine lakes fed by everlasting snows. Thousands of these little lakes, with deep, cold, emerald waters, are embosomed among the crags of the Rocky Mountains. These streams, born in the cold, gloomy solitudes of the upper mountain region, have a strange, eventful history as they pass down through gorges, tumbling in cascades and cataracts, until they reach the hot, arid plains of the Little Colorado, where the waters that were so clear above empty as turbid floods into the Gulf of California. . . .

Consider the action of one of these streams. Its source is in the mountains, where the snows fall; its course, through the arid plains. Now, if, at the river's flood, storms were falling on the plains, its channel would be cut but little faster than the adjacent country would be washed, and the general level would thus be preserved; but under the conditions here mentioned, the river continually deepens its beds; so all the streams cut deeper and still deeper, until their banks are towering cliffs of solid rock. These deep, narrow gorges are called canyons.

For more than a thousand miles along its course the Colorado has cut for itself such a canyon; but at some few points where lateral streams join it, the canyon is broken, and these narrow, transverse valleys divide it into a series of canyons.

Since the completion of the Glen Canyon dam in 1963 above the entrance of the Colorado into the Grand Canyon, the river has been altered: its wildness has been tamed, its flow controlled, and its sediment diminished; its muddy redness is gone, except when its canyon tributaries pour their flooded silted waters into it. But the extent of the river, its water supply, the character of its load, and its declivity are basically unaltered since Dutton described them almost a century ago:

Nature and Extent of the Water Supply of the Colorado

The upper tributaries of this river* have their sources in lofty regions which are abundantly watered. But the trunk river itself and its lower tributaries, and also the lower portions of the Green and Grand Rivers, flow through regions which are exceedingly arid. Of the body of water which flows through the Grand Canyon all but a small portion comes from the far distant highlands. The quantity contributed by the middle regions is very small. Although there are numberless waterways opening into the great chain of canyons, only a very few of them carry perennial streams, and these few living streams are mostly very small. The remainder, constituting by far the greater number of tributary chasms, convey spasmodic floods for a few days or hours at a time when the snows are melting, or when the infrequent showers and storms prevail. The river, however, receives accessions to its volume of water in the following manner. The country traversed by its middle courses is deeply scored with a vast number of profound side canyons, and the main stream itself flows at a depth varying from one thousand to six thousand feet below the general surface of the adjoining country. The

*Mr. Henry Gannett, geographer of the census, makes the total area of the drainage system of the Colorado 255,049 square miles, being second in extent of all the rivers of the United States which reach the ocean. That part of this drainage area which lies above the Grand Wash is given roughly at 165,000 square miles.

water which falls upon the country is in great part absorbed by the rocks and sinks into the depths, where no doubt it finds subterranean channels. Surface springs are exceedingly rare, but in the depths of the main chasm and in the bottoms of the side chasms near the river the springs are plentiful, and in many cases very copious, sending forth clear sparkling waters, beautiful to the sight, but sometimes heavily charged with obnoxious salts. In the Grand Canyon especially are many springs of water, and not a few considerable streams of large volume emerging from the rocks in the lower depths. Most of them are good and fresh, and a few are saline and hot. The body of water thus supplied to the river is quite considerable, and it is important here to note the fact that it brings no sediment.

Between the junction of the Green and Grand and the lower end of the Grand Canyon—a distance of about five hundred miles—the Colorado has only two tributaries, which bring into it considerable bodies of water, and which at the same time run in the open air, as distinguished from subterranean streams. These are the San Juan and Little Colorado. The volumes of these rivers at their confluences . . . during the greater portion of the year . . . are quite notable. They also bring great quantities of mud, sand, and gravel. Both enter the left bank of the river. All the other living streams are very small—in fact, mere rills—except at the times of irregular floods. On the other hand, the evaporation of the water in this part of the river in summertime must be very great. The dryness of the air is extreme and the heat intense. In June, July, August, and September the midday temperature of the air is seldom below 90°, and often exceeds 110° Fahrenheit, while the relative humidity is only from 0.3 to 0.4 of saturation. Still the river probably receives more water from the springs in the canyons and from the two larger tributaries than it loses by evaporation. . . . Much importance is here attached to the fact that this increase in the volume of the stream in the canyons consists largely of the water wholly free from sediment. It means an increase of transporting power in the river without an equivalent increase in the amount of material to be transported. The quantity of water which the Colorado carries varies, of course, enormously from season to season throughout the year. . . .

Origin and Character of the Load To Be Transported

We may now turn our attention to the material brought into the canyons constituting the load to be transported. Although the Colorado is a river which derives the greater part of its water and transported material from lofty regions at a great distance from the canyons, it still receives a notable amount of sediment from the Plateau Country contiguous to its banks. And it is interesting to note the conditions under which this sediment is contributed. The region adjoining the great canyons of the Colorado is so arid that it does not give rise to a single surface stream. The very few tributaries to the canyons, which carry water enough to be worthy of notice, have their sources far away in much loftier and moister countries. . . . Rains sufficiently copious to saturate the soil and set the gulches running are very infrequent and, perhaps, do not occur oftener than half a dozen times every year. But when they do come the consequences are very striking. The rills and washes are thick with mud and sand, and the water is loaded to its utmost capacity. There is no vegetation to form a sod and hold the earthy matters in their place. The instant a rill forms, it is a rill of mud. The country being scored with numberless canyons and steeply sloping gulches, the rills and streams are gathered together with marvelous rapidity and plunge furiously into these narrow chasms, where they rush along with prodigious velocity. The traveler in such a canyon who is admonished of the coming of a storm cannot be too diligent in seeking a place of safety. The murmur of the falling rain is followed in an incredibly short time by the deafening roar of the torrent, which rolls madly down the chasm as if some great reservoir above had burst its dam and discharged its waters. As it moves onward it sweeps everything loose in its way. Huge fragments of tons weight fallen from the cliffs above are bowled along with a facility that is highly suggestive. The water is charged to its utmost capacity with fine sand and silt, and it is somewhat surprising to see how much of this stuff a given quantity of water can carry. In the Mesozoic rocks it would not be an improbable estimate to say that these spasmodic waters carry nearly three times their own volume of fine material, and it is quite certain that they often carry more than twice their volume. Every explorer in this region can recite experiences of trying to obtain from some of the rills water for camp use by allowing a kettlefull to stand over night in order to settle, and finding in the morning an inch or two of dubious water on the surface of the vessel, with seven or eight inches of viscous red clay beneath and three or four inches of sand and grit at the bottom. The sediment thus transported is sand and clay. The rocks of the Mesozoic system are composed almost wholly of these two materials, the calcareous members being very few and of very small thickness; and such of the latter as occur are more frequently gypsum than calcite. The Permian also is similarly constituted, though having a few notable bands of arenaceous limestone. The cementing material of the sandy-clayey beds of the Trias and Permian is more or less gypsiferous, and many of the layers are highly charged with selenite. The ready solution of this cement yields an abundance of sand and clay in highly comminuted form, and every copious shower washes it along in great quantity.

The amount of this finer material which reaches the Colorado in the canyons is very great; and what is most striking, the contributions are not extremely irregular. In the summertime local showers, though infrequent in any given locality, are frequent enough in this portion of the Plateau Country as a whole. From any commanding point, which overlooks a very great expanse, distant showers may be seen on very many days of the hot summer. If we were to spend a week on such a point we might reckon with a high degree of probability upon one or more days in which heavy showers would be visible in different parts of the panorama. They are, however, extremely local, and rarely cover such large extents of country as the thunderstorms of the eastern states. It is not at all uncommon to see the rain streaks descending from a small cloud and falling upon areas no greater than three or four square miles. Still more curious is the formation of rain streaks without any cloud. When the season is showery many of the showers fail to reach the earth, the rain being completely re-evaporated in mid-air. It may thus be inferred that while rain is formed in the air daily throughout this region, only a small portion of it reaches the earth in showers sufficiently copious to saturate the soil and set the channels awash. Still, in an ordinary summer, a great majority of the days are somewhere marked with showers of sufficient volume to start the arroyos and canyons and pour a *debacle* of mud and sand into the Colorado. The river itself is rarely clear and is rarely otherwise than turbid and muddy. In the latter part of September and early part of October, the river is in some years quite clear and, at its lowest stage of water, displays that beautiful pistachio-green color which is seen in the waters of Niagara below the falls. At this season showers are infrequent. In the latter part of October, or in November, a rain storm, lasting from two or three to eight or ten days, may be looked for, and indeed rarely fails. It overspreads the entire region, and though the precipitation is not usually very copious on an average, yet it is so in many localities, and is always sufficient to flood many canyons which are normally dry, and to raise the water in the river very considerably. Immense quantities of sand and silt are then washed into the river, which is sometimes overburdened temporarily with sediment.

The greater part of the precipitation takes place in the winter months. Its amount varies more with the altitudes of the localities than with any other cause. Upon the higher levels it falls almost wholly as snow, and is usually very considerable. On the Kaibab the snow is always very heavy. Upon the lower and middle levels the precipitation in winter is more irregular when different years are compared. One year will furnish a heavy snowfall; another year will yield only a small amount of rain.

Rainfall and Declivity

While the precipitation upon the middle and lower levels—five thousand to sixty-five hundred feet above the sea—is on the whole quite small, the transporting power of such water as runs into the river is very great. A cubic yard of running water in the Plateau Country probably carries several times more sediment than the same quantity of water in the Atlantic rivers. This remarkable difference is due to the following causes: In the first place the soil and comminuted debris of the plateaus is not held together by vegetation, but lies loosely upon the rocks and taluses, and is easily gathered up by rills. But chiefly the slopes are always very great, and as the transporting power increases enormously with the declivity the only limit to the quantity of material a given volume of water can carry is reached when the mixture becomes so viscous that its own internal friction is great enough to seriously retard its rate of motion. In the rivers which drain the Appalachian region the finer material is supplied in quantity insufficient to load the running waters to their full capacity, while the rainfall is very copious and the declivities considerable. In the prairies of the Mississippi Valley the declivities are small, while the water supply is great and the finer material superabundant. In the plateaus the water supply is small, while the declivities are very great and the fine material also is relatively in excess. This will sufficiently explain why the spasmodic streams of the plateaus are so much more heavily loaded with sediment than those of moister regions.

The Declivity of the River

The declivity of the Colorado in the Grand Canyon next requires our attention. Between the junction of the Little Colorado and the Grand Wash the absolute altitude of the river bed declines from 2,640 to 1,000 feet above the sea—a total fall of 1,640 feet. The distance measured along the median line of the water surface is 218 miles, giving an average fall of 7.56 feet per mile. But the rate of descent through the various parts of the Canyon varies considerably. . . . Moreover, the fall is very unequal in the various parts of the [river]. . . . The entire extent of the river within the Canyon is a succession alternately of smooth reaches, with very small declivity, and swift rapids where the declivity is very great. In the Kaibab the smooth reaches are short, while the rapids are long and of great descent. . . . By comparing the distribution of fall with the nature of the rocks through which the river runs, it appears very clearly that the greater declivities occur in the Archæan rocks. . . . The Archæan rocks are, as a rule, much harder and are corraded with more difficulty than the others, and to this more obdurate character the greater declivities may be traced.

The rapids are, however, the results of two independent causes. (1) When the course of the stream lies in the hard rocks the rate of declivity is greater. The explanation is obvious. (2) The second cause is of a totally distinct nature. At the opening of every lateral chasm or side gorge a pile of rocks and rubble is thrown out into the main stream. Most of these side gorges are dry throughout the greater part of the year. But when the rains come their narrow beds are occupied with floods of muddy water, rushing downward with great velocity and often in great volume, bowling along fragments of all sizes from a few pounds to many tons. Thus an obstruction like a low dam is built across the river. The declivity of the side gorges is always much greater than that of the main stream. Their slopes are rarely less than two hundred feet to the mile. . . . The minimum slopes of the beds of the great amphitheaters in the Kaibab are seldom so small as two hundred feet to the mile. The power of a great flood rushing down such slopes is indeed formidable. When the torrents reach the river the larger fragments are dropped; for the maximum slope of the main stream (reckoned throughout any stretch exceeding four or five miles in length) never exceeds twenty-five feet to the mile, and the water, though enormous in volume at floodtime, has less velocity than the torrents of the side chasms. The river has, however, sufficient power to sweep onward masses of considerable size, which are rapidly ground up as they are rolled along.

It is apparent that in the work of corrasion an important part consists of the work of grinding up and destroying the masses which are brought into the main chasm by the spasmodic floods in the side gorges. Indeed, this constitutes by far the greatest part of the entire work. The coarse material—the large rocks, boulders, and rubble which pile up at the mouth of the lateral chasm—are gradually spread out below the dam, and the tendency is to build up and increase the grade of the smoother reach below. But this tendency is quickly checked and brought to a stop by the increased power of the main current due to the increased slope. The body of fragments thus rolled in is of great amount in the aggregate. On the whole, the amount at the present epoch is not sufficient to prevent the river from cutting down its channel, though the process is of course greatly retarded. The river is still sinking its chasm in the strata. There are many stretches of comparatively still water where there is an equilibrium between the tendency to cut still deeper, and the tendency to build up the bottom by the accumulation of debris. But a great part of the river bed is in the bare rock of the Paleozoic and Archæan strata, and wherever it is so the corrasion is proceeding at a rapid rate. Still other cases occur where the rate of corrasion is retarded but not completely counterbalanced by the accumulation, and these no doubt constitute the greater part of the extent of the chasm.

The great corrasive power of the Colorado is due to the large quantity of sand which it carries, and the high velocity given to its waters by its great declivity. As we have already shown, the quantity of fine material brought into the canyons is very large and the supply is almost continuous throughout the year. . . . A river may be powerless to corrade when its waters carry no sediment, and also when the sediment is so excessive that it cannot transport the entire supply. Neither of these extremes is found in the Colorado. The waters are heavily charged but not overloaded.

Sunset

The Canyon's pageant of beauty reaches its climax at sunset. All its multicolored temples are then radiant with vivid color. A canyon sunset may be an elemental experience as the purple canyon depths in slow ascent surround the shining temples until only their flaming peaks are visible—and the final burning glow is extinguished.

My most moving sunset visions have been at Hopi: the ensemble of peaks deepening their flaming intensity as the sea of darkness rises to engulf them.

And John Muir summed up the sunset climax in *The Century Magazine:*

Nature has a few big places beyond man's power to spoil—the ocean, the two icy ends of the globe, and the Grand Canyon. . . . The view down the gulf of color and over the rim of its wonderful wall, more than any other view I know, leads us to think of our earth as a star with stars swimming in light, every radiant spire pointing the way to the heavens. . . . One's most extravagant expectations are infinitely surpassed, though one expects much from what is said of it. . . . This is the main master furrow of its kind on our continent, incomparably greater and more impressive than any other yet discovered, or likely to be discovered.

II THE PHOTOGRAPHS

SUNRISE

THE joyous pageant of sunrise at the Canyon is unveiled from second to second, light leaping from peak to peak, transforming the world from darkness to the exultation of colorful, shining cliffs and temples.

From the Introduction

1 Hopi Point

I see the spectacle of morning . . . from daybreak to sunrise, with emotions an angel might share . . . I seem to partake its rapid transformation . . . enchantment reaches me. (EMERSON)

As sunrise unveils the canyon's depths and complex forms, what was flat and featureless becomes subtly and boldly sculptured. The change may be gradual or sudden. At times, however, the canyon's forms are barely visible, as cloud-darkened skies hold back the rays of sunlight. Such skies are often most impressive just before a storm—as if nature were intoxicating man with her beauty before dominating him with her power. A few minutes after this picture was taken, a furious storm had darkened the sky and was raging through the Canyon.

2   Hopi Point

This stillness, solitude, wildness of nature is . . . what I go out to seek. It is as if I always met in those places some grand, serene, immortal, infinitely encouraging, though invisible companion, and walked with him.   (THOREAU)

Hopi Point, the most popular sunset viewpoint, is also a sunrise favorite, lending itself to diverse panoramic effects. These are not usually best perceived, however, from within the point. The cliff ledges to the east of the point permit the photographer greater choice of composition. Results still are unpredictable, however, whether the photographer has aimed his camera at the most attractive scene or in the opposite direction. Anticipation may be one of the photographer's most useful tools, but it is often no match for nature's surprises.

3 Mather Point

Hail! Holy light, offspring of heaven, first born.
(JOHN MILTON, *Paradise Lost*)

The beauty of sunrise is not always easily available. To capture it with the camera may require patience or quickness or both. The rising of the sun may be so obscured by heavy clouds that nothing shows but a general dull lightening of the atmosphere. But waiting may reveal a lifting of the dulling clouds, and an almost instantaneous photographic response to the fleeting scene may seize a moment of beauty, as sunrise, from above Vishnu Temple, throws its shafts of light.

4 Hopi Point

*The morning wind forever blows, the poem of creation is uninterrupted;
but few are the ears that hear it.* (THOREAU)

Some of my most memorable experiences have been momentary explosions of beauty in the course of arid stretches of gray, dull scenes. On this November morning, sunrise seemed fated to celebrate nothing but leaden skies when a sudden burst of sunlight through heavy clouds illumined the scene.

5   Hopi Point

Behold, the bush burned with fire, and the bush was not consumed.

(EXODUS)

Sunrise at the Canyon on a stormy morning, with darkness unrelieved by brightening rays, can be disappointing. One waits, frustrated and often without success, for light to vivify a scene. With luck, a scene sometimes comes to momentary life. And with quick changes of lenses, filters, exposure valuation, and composition, the scene may be satisfyingly envisioned and seized.

6   Hopi Point

A man must attend to nature closely for many years to know when, as well as where, to look for his objects, since he must always anticipate her a little.   (THOREAU)

At Hopi Point, sunrise needs no special demonstration by nature. This scene, to me, is a revelation of the extraordinary quality of the seemingly ordinary canyon aspect. One of my favorite constants in an uncertain world is serenely waiting for the light of any ordinary sunrise to exhibit its beauty.

7   Lipan Point

We cannot see anything until we are possessed with it, and then we can hardly see anything else.
(THOREAU)

There is a multitude of sculptured canyon forms. For every named butte and temple there are countless others, many equally interesting, constantly formed and re-formed by light, shadow, and color as the day progresses in the Canyon's "wilderness of rocks." Each shape, viewed in its optimum setting, may be beautiful. The spotlight of sunrise seems to search for perfections in the canyon depths. Between the dark Kaibab limestone foreground and the cool Colorado River background, Escalante Butte here displays its Supai color.

8   Mather Point

Sweet is the breath of Morn, her rising sweet,
. . . pleasant the sun,
When first on this delightful land he spreads
His orient beams. . .

(JOHN MILTON, Paradise Lost)

The canyon slopes, often useful for obtaining photographic vantage points, are, at times, also visually interesting, although usually less dramatic than the steep canyon cliffs. Here, just below the rim, decorated with fir trees (which grow only on the slopes below the rim at the Canyon South Rim), brilliant with fresh snow, is a winter sunrise view.

9   Moran Point

May I gird myself to be a hunter of the beautiful, that naught escape me! . . . I am eager to report the glory of the universe.   (THOREAU)

This memorable vision was a reward for valor beyond the normal call of photographic duty. The temperature had gone down to 27 degrees below zero during the night. My car clock had stopped, its moving parts frozen together. Some apples in the car, now icy mush, had shrunk to half their former size. I made the mistake of removing my hands from my gloves; when I put them back they were encased in ice, and hurt for two months after.

THE WEST RIM

Almost all the major canyon temples . . . have been eroded from the North Rim, but these are normally best viewed from the South Rim; unless they are seen from a distance, they lose much of their awesome aspect and complex configuration. . . . The West Rim (of the South Rim) offers the most intricate canyon perspectives. . . .

Only from the West Rim may one see the multitude of magnificent temples surrounding Bright Angel Canyon, arranged in infinitely varied patterns of form, color, light, and shadow.

From the Introduction

10 Mather Point, Panorama

Full many a glorious morning have I seen
Flatter the mountain tops with sovereign eye.
(SHAKESPEARE, *Sonnet XXXIII*)

The transition from sunrise to early morning light offers some of the most fascinating canyon perspectives. The Canyon stretches out broadly and deeply with multiple scenes of changing form and richly varied color. The eye sweeps across a profusion of shifting patterns. Perhaps such a scene as this inspired an early visitor to exclaim, "the marvelous sea of color was like the revelation of a new Jerusalem."

11   Mohave Point, Panorama

It is curious how a little obstacle becomes a great obstruction when a misstep would land a man in the bottom of a deep chasm. Climbing the face of a cliff, a man will without hesitancy walk along a step or a shelf but a few inches wide if the landing is but ten feet below, but if the foot of the cliff is a thousand feet down he will prefer to crawl along the shelf.   (J. W. POWELL)

Many observers are inclined to overlook the extreme variety of canyon views, not only from point to point, but even from any one point. An excellent photographer once advised me not to waste too much time at the Canyon, since it was all one relatively undifferentiated multicolored effect. To me, each point has its own individuality, of scene and mood. Mohave Point, especially, offers many different views. This scene, to the west of the point, was taken early one February morning.

12   Pima Point, Panorama

One must not think of a mountain range (in the Grand Canyon area) as a line of peaks standing on a plain, but as a broad platform many miles wide from which mountains have been carved by the waters.

(J. W. POWELL)

Pima Point, with the broadest West Rim panorama, offers its most interesting views from nearby cliff ledges. Caution is imperative, but composition is demanding. The Granite Gorge, often obscured, is here a shining embellishment for the Pima panorama of weird forms, sheer cliffs, knife-like ridges and grand temples.

13 Pima Point, Juniper Tree

In Wildness is the preservation of the World. Every tree sends its fibres forth in search of the Wild. . . . From the forest and wilderness come the tonics and barks which brace mankind. (THOREAU)

My favorite South Rim companion is the juniper tree, whether it enriches a panoramic scene or, as here, poses for its portrait on a sunny November afternoon.

14 Mather Point, Panorama

If I wished to see a mountain or other scenery under the most favorable auspices, I would go to it in foul weather, so as to be there when it cleared up; we are then in the most suitable mood, and nature is most fresh and inspiring. There is no serenity so fair as that which is just established in a tearful eye.

(THOREAU)

Delicious sunshine . . . contrasted strangely with the wild tones of the storm. (MUIR)

One of my vivid canyon memories is of the snowstorm here seen retreating toward the North Rim. I had watched the storm approaching for some time. The Canyon was dark and gloomy, the wind was howling, it was freezing cold, and the few visitors who braved the view took a quick look and ran. I waited, hoping that the storm would unveil some photogenic drama. The storm reached Mather, hurled some snow in my face for a few minutes, and then began to dissipate as it moved away. Suddenly the clouds parted and the setting sun poured its glow on the forms flanking Bright Angel Canyon.

15   Hopi Point, Panorama

Ah! I need solitude! . . . It is with infinite yearning and aspiration that I seek solitude . . . I have come forth to this hill at sunset to see the forms of the mountains . . . to commune with something grander than man.   (THOREAU)

Panoramic scenes do not always provide the most interesting views. Unless they present special features of form, color, or light they may be disappointing. Hopi Point, however, displays the very model of a panoramic scene, with an inexhaustible variety of effects. Here nature seems to say: feast your eyes!

16 Yavapai Point, Sumner Butte

One could almost imagine that the walls had been carved with a purpose, to represent giant architectural forms. (J. W. POWELL)

To perceive freshly, with fresh senses, is to be inspired. (THOREAU)

To complement the complexity of canyon panoramic patterns one needs the simplicity of individually portrayed form. The panorama at Yavapai Point makes it easy to focus on such portraits. In this view Sumner Butte, directly above the Colorado River and east of Bright Angel Creek, rises above the glowing Granite Gorge.

17 Yavapai Point, Isis

The buttes . . . sometimes form very conspicuous features of a landscape and are of marvelous beauty by reason of their sculptured escarpments. Below they are often buttressed on a magnificent scale. Softer beds give rise to a vertical structure of buttresses and columns, while the harder strata appear in great horizontal lines, suggesting architectural entablature. Then the strata of which these buttes are composed are of many vivid colors; so color and form unite in producing architectural effects, and the buttes often appear like Cyclopean temples.   (J. W. POWELL)

This scene represents to me one of the basic symbols of Grand Canyon beauty—the simple majesty of the temple of Isis crowning a complex but beautifully patterned series of elaborately sculptured forms, all enriched with deep color and glowing light.

THE EAST RIM

T HE East Rim is a land of sweeping vistas and enchanting color. The fantastic array of Bright Angel temples no longer dominates the scene, but forms the background for some of its broad panoramas. The great canyon walls and temples still overwhelm the viewer, but the narrow, formidable Granite Gorge is here seen only from a distance; in its place is a broad valley formed by the mighty Colorado River here meandering in softer, tilted-rock formations . . . here laid bare, displaying the most brilliant canyon colors. . . . Viewed from Lipan Point, especially, the crimson hues are unusually vivid.

From the Introduction

18   Grandview Point, Panorama

The elements with which the walls are constructed, from black buttress below to alabaster tower above . . . weather in different forms and are painted in different colors.   (J. W. POWELL)

Grandview, earliest of favored canyon viewpoints, combines the intimacy of individual rocks and trees, the sweep of canyon form in depth, and distant temples in many broad panoramas. This view was obtained from a ledge about fifty feet below the canyon rim.

19   Grandview Point, Panorama

Morn . . . with rosy hand
Unbarr'd the gates of light.
(JOHN MILTON, *Paradise Lost*)

One of the joys of mountain photography is imagining the possible beauty of an image never seen. Having seen this view late one afternoon, when it lacked special appeal, I was drawn to it at daybreak the next morning, and was rewarded with a "painted" Canyon to match the Painted Desert, which appears in the distance.

20 Moran Point, Panorama

Let every eye negotiate for itself,
And trust no agent; for beauty is a witch,
Against whose charms faith melteth into blood.
(SHAKESPEARE, *Much Ado About Nothing*)

There is, perhaps, no more familiar canyon scene than this, which adorns the canyon's stationery. But no matter how often the scene is pictured, more remains to be expressed. Each season of the year, of course, reveals different tones of light and color. Here it is portrayed, midmorning, on a crisp winter day.

21 Moran Point, Juniper Tree

Nature does not cast pearls before swine. There is just as much beauty visible to us in the landscape as we are prepared to appreciate, not a grain more.   (THOREAU)

In short, all good things are wild and free.   (THOREAU)

The canyon junipers are fitting companions for both the viewer and the scene they complement. This juniper, my favorite, unimpressive from the rim, is seen to advantage from the slope about ten feet below. Growing out of rocky soil, exposed to cold, contorted by wind, stripped of its lovely foliage, it seems to say:

> They also serve who only stand
> and proudly
> and joyously
> struggle to endure.

22 Lipan Point, Panorama

The details of structure can be seen only at close view, but grand effects of structure can be witnessed in great panoramic scenes. Seen in detail, gorges and precipices appear; seen at a distance, in comprehensive views, vast massive structures are presented. The traveler on the brink looks from afar and is overwhelmed with the sublimity of massive forms. (J. W. POWELL)

Perhaps nowhere else at the Canyon may the viewer enjoy as wide a variety of spectacular scenic effects as at Lipan Point, which offers broad views to both east and west as well as across the Canyon, and displays the Colorado River in its meandering entrance into the Canyon from the east and its dramatic disappearance into the Granite Gorge to the west. This view, looking west, was taken on a bright winter morning.

23 Lipan Point, Canyon Depths

The streams that head far back on the plateau on either side come down in gorges and break the wall into sections. . . . That which has been described as a wall is such only in its grand effect. In detail it is a series of structures separated by a ramification of canyons, each having its own walls.   (J. W. POWELL)

At Lipan Point one is privileged to see and feel an intimate and dramatic demonstration of the evolution of the earth and of life itself. Beneath one's feet are the fossil shell fragments of ancient marine life, imbedded in the Kaibab limestone—and in the distance, as in this view, one seems to witness the Granite Gorge rising out of the earth, with the Colorado River cutting into the pre-biologic rock.

24   Lipan Point, Venus and Apollo

I fall back onto visions which I have had. What else adds to my possessions and makes me rich in all lands? If you have ever done any work with these finest tools, the imagination and fancy and reason, it is a new creation, independent of the world, and a possession forever.   (THOREAU)

In this scene the complexities of canyon form are dominated by the union of the temples of Venus and Apollo, as the Colorado River curves below—all warmed by the deep tones of a winter sunset.

25 Desert View, Panorama

In Nature . . . is constant surprise and novelty . . . each day's feast in Nature's year is a surprise to us and adapted to our appetite and our spirits. She has arranged such an order of feasts as never tires.

(THOREAU)

The Painted Desert, the flat background of the picture, seems misnamed, viewed from this distance. But the Canyon before it, under proper lighting, offers all sorts of "painted" perspectives, as the winding Colorado River contrasts and blends with its complementary surroundings.

THE NORTH RIM

THE traveler from the South Rim . . . finds the lovely North Rim wilderness a refreshment to a somewhat parched soul. Its spruces, firs, and pines . . . are splendidly displayed in open, soaring variety of form, texture, and shades of cooling green.

The special glory of this coniferous forest, however, is the profusion of aspens, yellow-green in the spring and gold sprinkled with orange and red in the fall.

The Canyon itself, here as at the South Rim, is an overwhelming experience. . . . In addition, one may discover unsuspected beauty in the temples familiar from South Rim viewing.

From the Introduction

26 Aspens, Road to Cape Royal

October is the month for painted leaves. Their rich glow now flashes round the world.   (THOREAU)

These little leaves are the stained windows in the cathedral of my world.   (THOREAU)

I was searching for aspens that would be more than splashes of gold in the green hillsides, or shapely trunks posing in stately elegance. The shifting light and deficiencies of form or color were disappointing, and I had almost given up hope, one October morning, when I caught this image out of the corner of my eye.

27 Cape Royal, Vishnu Temple

As we mount the parapet which looks down upon the Canyon the eye is at once caught by an object which seems to surpass in beauty anything we have yet seen. It is a gigantic butte, so admirably designed and so exquisitely decorated that the sight of it must call forth an expression of wonder and delight from the most apathetic beholder. Its summit is more than five thousand feet above the river. . . . We named it VISHNU'S TEMPLE.   (DUTTON)

Perhaps the most conspicuous of all canyon temples is Vishnu. It is probably visible from more South Rim viewpoints than any other grand form except its companion, Wotan's Throne. From the South Rim, however, it is usually a graceful, pointed dome. From Cape Royal, where it seems almost close enought to touch, it rises dramatically, an imposing mass.

28 Point Imperial, Mount Hayden

All the phenomena of nature need to be seen from the point of view of wonder and awe.   (THOREAU)

I feel
The link of nature draw me: flesh of flesh,
Bone of my bone thou art, and from thy state
Mine never shall be parted, bliss or woe.
(JOHN MILTON, *Paradise Lost*)

The panorama from Point Imperial justifies its name, but its most spectacular form is Mount Hayden, named for the pioneer geologist. Seen in midafternoon, sculptured by light and shadow, Mount Hayden is impressively regal. My favorite view, however, is shortly before sunset, when it is displayed in deep, bold relief.

29 Cape Royal, Wotan's Throne, Sunrise

If by patience, if by watching, I can secure one new ray of light, can feel myself elevated for an instant upon Pisgah, the world which was dead prose to me become living and divine, shall I not watch ever? . . . We are surrounded by a rich and fertile mystery. May we not probe it, pry into it, employ ourselves about it, a little? To devote your life to the discovery of the divinity in nature. . . . (THOREAU)

In presenting man with her great mountain spectacles, nature is rather capricious. There are some great forms that are seen to advantage at limited times—some at sunset or sunrise only, some only in the middle of the day. But nature also has her visual favorites, day-long beneficiaries of the play of light and shadow, which are constantly on beautiful display. Wotan's Throne, from Cape Royal, is one of these. The progression of the sun yields one fascinating view after another. The middle of the day best portrays the temple as a whole, but my preferred views are at sunrise and sunset, when the cliffs reflect the warmest light of day with grandeur and enchantment. To capture the vision of this picture, to see it most dramatically and to feel it most deeply, it is necessary to stand at the very edge of the point.

30 Cape Royal, Wotan's Throne, Sunset

I will take another walk to the cliff . . . There I am at home. In the . . . crust of the earth I recognize my friend.   (THOREAU)

The setting sun . . . with amber light . . . seemed to say . . . "My peace I give unto you."
(MUIR)

Sunrise at Cape Royal displays the outer wall of Wotan's Throne. At sunset the inner cliff is revealed, isolated by shadow and warmed by light.

FORMATIONS AND FORMS

Each formation has its own special beauty. . . . The varieties of . . . formation would be fascinating enough if they were all of one color. (The creamy Kaibab limestone, by itself, is a dazzling reflector of the bright gleam of sunrise and the deep glow of sunset.) But their basic effect stems from the rainbow hues which transform them—above all, the crimson glow that often floods the canyon chasm.

From the Introduction

31 Mather Point, Kaibab Pillars

The most sweet and tender, the most innocent and encouraging society may be found in any natural object. (THOREAU)

Some of the most intriguing canyon forms seem to be constantly looked at but rarely seen—if one can judge from the apparent inattention of viewers and photographers. As Dutton said, "Why one form should be beautiful and another unattractive; why one should be powerful, animated and suggestive, while another is meaningless, are questions for the metaphysician rather than the geologist." Perhaps the artist can aid the metaphysician. These pillars, gently glowing at sunrise, are posing at the most popular spot on the most visited canyon viewpoint.

32 Mather Point, Kaibab Fantasy

The finest workers in stone are not copper or steel tools, but the gentle touches of air and water working at their leisure with a liberal allowance of time.   (THOREAU)

Just below the pillars of the preceding picture is my favorite of all the canyon minor forms. Intricately carved out of Kaibab limestone, it here displays its winter sunrise aspect.

33   Mather Point, Kaibab Wall

In the morning everything is joyous and bright . . . every pulse beats high, every life-cell rejoices, the very rocks seem to tingle with life.   (MUIR)

Mather is really a series of points, from each of which the Kaibab wall of the nearest point may be easily viewed. Sunrise at Mather thus offers a variety of glowing cliffs—all to be enjoyed in thrilling, quick succession, if one hurriedly moves from point to point.

34 Lipan Point, Coconino Wall

If a stone appeals to me and elevates me . . . it is a matter of private rejoicing.   (THOREAU)

One of the innumerable manifestations of the grandeur of the canyon is the shapely, massive profile of a Coconino sandstone wall. A telephoto lens is often an invaluable aid in capturing its simple majesty, here adorned by winter sunrise.

35 Powell Point, Coconino Cliff

There is in my nature, methinks, a singular yearning toward all wildness. I know of no redeeming qualities in myself but a sincere love for some things. (THOREAU)

Viewed from a distance, as at Lipan Point, the Coconino sandstone is a stable, imposing mass. Viewed from almost directly above, the eye plunging steeply down its precipitous cliff into the canyon depths, it is a dynamic thrust. Seen here is a part of the cliff below Hopi Point, viewed from the edge of the Powell Point cliff.

36 Lipan Point, Supai Slope

When thinking of these rocks one must not conceive of piles of boulders or heaps of fragments, but of a whole land of naked rock, with giant forms carved on it: cathedral-shaped buttes, towering hundreds or thousands of feet, cliffs that cannot be scaled, and canyon walls that shrink the river into insignificance.

(J. W. POWELL)

There are times when perception is swamped by a multitude of attractions. At Lipan Point one may easily be distracted by a succession of diverse scenes. Some of the most interesting, such as this Supai slope of Escalante Butte, are often overlooked.

37   Moran Point, Kaibab Pillar

Surely joy is the condition of life.
(THOREAU)

Not all the great pillars of the Canyon are without recognition. This massive form plays a featured role in one of the most familiar of all canyon scenes, the Colorado River panorama from Moran Point. On an almost unbearably cold winter morning it deserved intensity of concentration.

38　Hopi Point, Kaibab Cliff

One day the sun shall shine more brightly than ever he has done, shall perchance shine into our minds and hearts, and light up our whole lives with a great awakening light.　(THOREAU)

This is a close-up vision of one of my favorite canyon cliffs, blazing with winter sunrise. To capture it properly, one must walk east of Hopi Point to a projecting ledge—which might be dangerous to an unwary or overabsorbed photographer.

THE COLORADO RIVER

THE Colorado River . . . the most impressive rock-carving tool in the history of the earth . . . is also a festival of beauty, with myriad shapes, colors, and settings.

It may be an arrow . . . as seen from Lipan; a stately bend at Pima; a graceful ribbon at Moran; a sinuous whip near Desert View, or a voluptuous curve at Lipan.

At times . . . red . . . it is now normally blue or green. . . . In the west, the Colorado displays its beauty beneath the massive Granite Gorge. In the east, the Colorado's lovely blues and greens wind their graceful way through banks of red and purple.

From the Introduction

39 Mohave Point

This curious world which we inhabit is more wonderful than it is convenient; more beautiful than it is useful . . . more to be admired and enjoyed than used.   (THOREAU)

The Colorado River, second in size only to the Mississippi in this country, has little commercial value. It seems fitting that the "profitless" Canyon should have its beauty enhanced by an equally "profitless" river. At Mohave Point the Colorado, which is often concealed from West Rim view by the steep and narrow Granite Gorge, is well displayed from the west side of the point, as it curves around the Gorge on its way to the Gulf of California.

40 Pima Point

A river is best seen breaking through highlands, issuing from some narrow pass. It imparts a sense of power. (THOREAU)

This scene portrays the results of two extremely different aspects of nature's power: first, her sudden, furious outbursts—storms flooding the gorge of Monument Creek and pouring massive boulders into the Colorado to form the Granite Rapids below; and, second, her gradual, irresistible force—as the unceasing Colorado patiently but relentlessly cuts into the tough but ultimately yielding Granite Gorge.

41 Yavapai Point

A precipitous wall of mountain rises over the river, with crag and pinnacle and cliff in black and brown, and through it runs an angular pattern of red and gray dikes of granite.   (J. W. POWELL)

What often distinguishes this scene for viewers is the bridge across the Colorado below. To me, it is the most majestic setting of the river in the Canyon. Here the warming early light enriches the foreground Tonto Plateau, the mid-picture Supai-topped butte, and the rugged Granite Gorge.

42 Moran Point

The landscape everywhere, away from the river, is of rock—cliffs of rock, tables of rock, plateaus of rock, terraces of rock, crags of rock—ten thousand strangely carved forms; rocks everywhere, and no vegetation, no soil, no sand. In long, gentle curves the river winds about these rocks. (J. W. POWELL)

Sometimes a scene attracts a photographer primarily for its form, or its color, or its texture, or its light and shadow, or its depth—or, as here, for a combination of them all. It is hardly surprising that this point is named for the distinguished American painter of the West, Thomas Moran.

43   Lipan Point

The river meanders in great curves . . . in passing down the canyon it seems to be enclosed by walls, but oftener by . . . towering structures.   (J. W. POWELL)

At Lipan Point, the Colorado displays its beauty in many spectacular settings. Viewed toward the west, it may be seen gradually cutting its way into the Granite Gorge. Viewed toward the east, as here on a winter morning, it seems to be wandering through gently sloping colored banks.

44 Lipan Point

A hidden light illumines all our seeing,
An unknown love enchants our solitude.
We feel and know that from the depths of being
Exhales an infinite, a perfect good.

(SANTAYANA)

This previously uncelebrated section of the Colorado River is one of my favorite canyon scenes. The picture represents the culmination of over an hour of waiting and watching, as shifting clouds formed and re-formed a constantly, split-second, changing scene, until suddenly the decisive moment arrived.

45   Lipan Point

What better comfort have we, or what other profit
                                          in living,
Than to feed, sobered by the truth of Nature,
Awhile upon her bounty and her beauty,
And hand her torch of gladness to the ages
                                          following after?

(SANTAYANA)

This scene represents a challenge to the photographer. It is easy to display its obvious form and color. It is difficult to do justice to its combination of classic and baroque qualities.

46 Desert View

The rivers now, those great blue subterranean heavens, reflecting the supernal skies. (THOREAU)

It is fitting that a great performer should make a great entrance. The pageant of Colorado River beauty at the Canyon starts at Desert View, where the Colorado leaves the Palisades of the desert to enter the Canyon proper. Desert View itself provides some excellent viewpoints. Slightly to the west of Desert View, however, there is a turnout, ignored by most visitors, which provides an unusually attractive perspective, especially, as in this picture, with a telephoto lens.

SUNSET

THE Canyon's pageant of beauty reaches its climax at sunset. All its multicolored temples are then radiant with vivid color. A canyon sunset may be an elemental experience as the purple canyon depths in slow ascent surround the shining temples until only their flaming peaks are visible—and the final burning glow is extinguished.

From the Introduction

47   Desert View

Live in each season as it passes . . . breathe the air, drink the drink, taste the fruit, and resign yourself to the influences of each . . . Grow green with spring, yellow and ripe with autumn.   (THOREAU)

It may seem paradoxical, but one of the joys of solitude is the reflection that the scene that now absorbs the viewer is shared with those who were here before he came and with those who will be here after he goes. The Watchtower, a replica of an Indian structure that includes a ceremonial chamber—linking us to our early American brothers—is viewed here in its autumn sunset colors.

48   Desert View

. . . the glorious sun
Stays in his course and plays the alchemist,
Turning with splendour of his precious eye
The meager cloddy earth to glittering gold.
                    (SHAKESPEARE, *King John*)

Some of the most beautiful canyon forms are inconspicuous during most of the day; hardly discernible as individual forms, they merge with the surrounding rock in one undifferentiated mass. At sunset, however, as here, they may emerge from their camouflaged obscurity, sculptured by darkening shadow, vibrant with warming light.

49   Desert View

Warmth, warmth, more warmth! for we are dying of cold and not of darkness.

(MIGUEL DE UNAMUNO)

Some of my most thrilling visual experiences have been as sudden as an explosion—others have been as gradual as the unfolding of the petals of a flower. At sunset you can watch the great cliff of the Palisades of the desert change almost imperceptibly as the sun paints the wall with gold, then orange, and, finally, blazing red.

50   Desert View

Death twitches my ear. "Live," he says, "I am coming."
(VIRGIL, as quoted by Justice
Oliver Wendell Holmes, in a radio address
on his ninetieth birthday)

Many of my pictures are planned in advance—sometimes years before I get the opportunity to take them. Others, such as this, are happy accidents. As I was about to leave Desert View late one winter afternoon, having apparently exhausted its special photographic possibilities, I walked along the rim west of the Watchtower to take one last look at the fading scene, when I caught a glimpse of this image and feverishly rushed to seize it.

51 Yavapai Point

As the sun draws near the horizon, the great drama of the day begins . . . stronger and sharper becomes the relief . . . a thousand forms . . . stand forth in strength and animation. All things seem to grow in beauty, power, and dimensions. What was grand before becomes majestic, the majestic becomes sublime, and . . . the sublime . . . transcendent.   (DUTTON)

Among the multitude of canyon forms, the majestic temples, properly posed, give the searching eye a chance to suspend its restless quest and to focus on a complexly integrated vision of varied shapes, colors, and tones of light, as in this portrait of the temple of Isis.

52 Yavapai Point

Was it a vision, or a waking dream?
Fled is that music:—Do I wake or sleep?
(JOHN KEATS, *Ode to a Nightingale*)

Sunset photography at Grand Canyon may yield some unanticipated results, as the declining sun shifts the angle of its light. On the West Rim, the deepening rays first reach the temples west of Bright Angel Canyon, but the final, warmest tones of crimson most richly affect the temples east of Bright Angel Canyon, notably, as here, Deva, Brahma, and Zoroaster temples.

53 Yavapai Point

We had a remarkable sunset one day . . . When we reflected that this was not a solitary phenomenon, but that it would happen forever an infinite number of evenings, and cheer and reassure the latest child that walked there, it was more glorious still. (THOREAU)

Canyon sunsets are not always melodramatic. At times gentle tones of light illumine the Canyon's immensity and decorate the brooding clouds.

54   Hopi Point

My profession is to be always on the alert to find God in nature, to know his lurking places, to attend all the oratorios, the operas, in nature.   (THOREAU)

This scene is just below Hopi Point, difficult to see, and even more difficult to photograph. My first view of this scene was accidental. I was turning away from viewing the temples in the distance when a glint of nearby light beneath me caught the corner of my eye. Taking a picture such as this involves some risk. It is prudent to make sure that one's footing is completely solid, and that the cliff-edge slope does not make balance precarious.

55 Hopi Point

*Open all your pores and bathe in all the tides of Nature, in all her streams and oceans, at all seasons
. . . For all nature is doing her best each moment to make us well. She exists for no other end. Do not resist
her.* (THOREAU)

Among the rewards of photography are unexpected delights. One November afternoon I was
waiting for the changing light to present a combined view of the temples of Isis and Buddha in a
unified pattern of form, color, light, and shadow. My hoped-for image never appeared, but as I
waited, glancing about for other possible views, this scene caught my eye.

56 Hopi Point

It was a splendid sunset that day, a celestial light on all the land . . . equally glorious in whatever quarter you looked.   (THOREAU)

This picture represents the realization of the image I failed to capture on the day I took the preceding picture. The temples of Isis and Buddha, mid-picture left, are posing as I hoped they would, unifying a complex canyon scene.

57   Hopi Point

All Nature's wildness tells the same story . . . each and all are the orderly beauty-making love-beats of Nature's heart.   (MUIR)

This scene had been covered with dark clouds for some time, with teasing glints of light occasionally suggesting possibilities of beauty, when suddenly the clouds parted, for a few seconds of searchlight illumination.

58   Hopi Point

The scene before me was awful, sublime, and glorious—awful in profound depths, sublime in massive and strange forms, and glorious in colors.   (J. W. POWELL)

This scene immediately followed the preceding scene—within a few seconds the view changed from dull to spectacular, and back to dull again. Within these critical seconds I managed to take just two pictures—this one and the one preceding.

59   Hopi Point

The true harvest of my daily life is somewhat as intangible and indescribable as the tints of morning or evening. It is a little star-dust caught, a segment of the rainbow which I have clutched.   (THOREAU)

The grandest picture in the world is the sunset sky.   (THOREAU)

The sunset scene had been disappointing up to the final seconds. Illumination was too scanty and fitful for enjoyable viewing or photography. But the setting of the sun, which seems to too many to be the finale to the beauty of the day, is often, as here, merely the prelude.

60   Yavapai Point

Men nowhere . . . live yet a natural life . . . [Man] needs not only be spiritualized, but naturalized, *on the soil of earth . . . Here or nowhere is our heaven.*   (THOREAU)

How can you live, strange souls that nothing awes?   (DE MUSSET, *translated by* SANTAYANA)

Taking this picture was an exciting experience. I had finished watching sunset at Hopi Point—there seemed little promise in the post-sunset sky—and I was driving back to Canyon Village when I suddenly saw a blaze of cloud in my rearview mirror. I raced to Yavapai Point, rushed up the hill to a cliff edge—simultaneously composing my picture, choosing my viewpoint, my foreground, my lens, and my exposure as I ran—rammed my tripod into a secure cliff hold, changed lenses and took my picture.

III APPENDIXES

Clarence E. Dutton on How the Grand Canyon Was Made

THE excavation of the Grand Canyon and the sculpture of its walls and buttes are the results of two processes acting in concert—corrasion and weathering. In discussing these processes it is necessary to take into the account the peculiar conditions under which they have operated, and these are chiefly the climate and the elevation of the country.

In common parlance it is customary to say that the river has cut its canyon. This expression states but a small portion of the truth. The river has in reality cut only a narrow trench, of which the width is equal to the width of the water surface. It has also been the vehicle which has carried away to another part of the world the materials that have been cut away by both processes. Opening laterally into the main chasm are many amphitheaters excavated back into the main platform of the country. At the bottom of each is a stream bed, over which in some cases a perennial river flows, while in other cases the water runs only during the rains. Like the trunk river itself, these streams, whether permanent or spasmodic, have cut down their channels to depths varying somewhat among themselves, but generally a little less than the depth of the central chasm. These tributaries often fork, and the forks are quite homologous to the tributaries in the foregoing respects. They, too, have cut narrow gashes no wider than their water surfaces. Down the faces of the walls and down the steep slopes of the taluses run myriads of rain gullies. When the rain comes it gathers into rills, which cascade down the wall clefts and rush headlong through the troughs in the talus. Carrying an abundance of sand and grit, the waters scour out these little channels in much the same way as their united streams and rills cut down their beds in the amphitheaters and in the main chasm itself. But the work of corrasion by running water is limited to the cutting of very narrow grooves in the rocks, the width of the cutting at any given time and place being equal to the width of the water surface of the stream. Corrasion alone, then, could never have made the Grand Canyon what it is. The amount of material removed by that process is but a very small fraction of the total excavation. Another process acting conjointly with the corrasion, and in an important sense dependent upon it, has effected by far the greater part of the destruction. This additional process is weathering. In order to comprehend the combined results of the two, it is necessary to study their action in detail.

Mr. G. K. Gilbert, in his excellent monograph *Geology of the Henry Mountains,* has embodied a chapter on "Land Sculpture," which sets forth, in most logical and condensed form, the mechanical principles which enter into the problems of erosion. In his comprehensive analysis may be found a discussion of the conditions under which the sculpturing forces and processes achieve such abnormal results as we observe in the Plateau Country. . . .

Mr. Gilbert's work:

> The mechanical wear of streams is performed by the aid of hard mineral fragments carried along by the current. The effective force is that of the current; the tools are mud, sand, and boulders. The most important of them is sand; it is chiefly by the impact and friction of grains of sand that the rocky beds of streams are disintegrated.
>
> Where a stream has all the load of a given degree of comminution which it is capable of carrying, the entire energy of the descending water and load is consumed in the translation of the water and load, and there is none applied to corrasion. If it has an excess of load its velocity is thereby diminished so as to lessen its competence, and a portion is dropped. If it has less than a full load, it is in condition to receive more, and it corrades its bottom. A fully loaded stream is on the verge between corrasion and deposition. . . . The work of transportation may thus monopolize a stream to the exclusion of corrasion, or the two works may be carried forward at the same time.
>
> The rapidity of the mechanical corrasion depends on the hardness, size, and number of transient fragments, on the hardness of the rock bed, and on the velocity of the stream. . . . The element of velocity is of double importance, since it determines not only the speed, but to a great extent the size of the pestles which grind the rocks. The coefficients upon which it in turn depends, namely, declivity and quantity of water, have the same importance in corrasion that they have in transportation.
>
> Let us suppose that a stream endowed with a constant volume of water is at some point continuously supplied with as great a load as it is capable of carrying. For so great a distance as its velocity remains the same it will neither corrade nor deposit, but will leave the declivity of its bed unchanged. But if in its progress it reaches a place where a lesser declivity of bed gives a diminished velocity, its capacity for transportation will become less than the load, and part of the load will be deposited; or if in its progress it reaches a place where a greater declivity of bed gives an increased velocity, the capacity for transportation will become greater than the load, and there will be corrasion of the bed. In this way a stream which has a supply of debris equal to its capacity tends to build up the gentler slopes of its bed and cut away the steeper. It tends to establish a single uniform grade.
>
> Let us now suppose that the stream, after having obliterated all the inequalities of the grade of its bed, loses nearly the whole of its load. Its velocity is at once accelerated, and vertical corrasion begins through its whole length. Since the stream has the same declivity, and consequently the same velocity at all points, its capacity for corrasion is everywhere the

same. Its rate of corrasion, however, will depend on the character of its bed. Where the rock is hard, corrasion will be less rapid than where it is soft, and there will result inequalities of grade. But as soon as there is inequality of grade there is inequality of velocity and inequality of capacity for corrasion; and where hard rocks have produced declivities, there the capacity for corrasion will be increased. The differentiation will proceed until the capacity for corrasion is everywhere proportioned to the resistance and no further; that is, until there is equilibrium of action.

In general, we may say that a stream tends to equalize its work in all parts of its course. Its power inheres in its fall, and each foot of fall has the same power. When its work is to corrade, and the resistance is unequal, it concentrates its energy where the resistance is great by crowding many feet of descent into a small space, and diffuses it where the resistance is small, by using but a small fall in a long distance. When its work is to transport, the resistance is constant and the fall is evenly distributed by a uniform grade. When its work includes both transportation and corrasion, as in the usual case, its grades are somewhat unequal, and the inequality is the greatest when the load is the least.

The foregoing analysis is applicable to the Colorado. Among the large rivers of the world considered as trunk streams draining large areas, its condition and operations are exceptional, though by no means wholly unique. Nearly all large rivers along their lower and middle courses and along considerable portions of the larger tributaries have reached or nearly approximated to that condition of equilibrium of action which Mr. Gilbert speaks of, in which the transporting power is nearly adjusted without excess to the load to be carried; and they have little or no tendency either to corrade or to deposit. But the Colorado is corrading rapidly, and has doubtless done so during a great part of its history. . . .

We have seen that the work of corrasion, pure and simple, is limited to the cutting of deep and narrow gashes in the strata and to the grinding up of the larger fragments brought into the channels. The widening of these cuts into the present configuration of the Canyon and the sculpture of the walls are the work of the process which is termed weathering. By far the greater part of the material removed in the total process of the excavation has been broken up and comminuted by the action of atmospheric reagents, and their mode of operation is worthy of careful study.

The peculiar cliff forms of the Grand Canyon, and indeed of the province at large, would hardly be possible in any other country, for no other country presents all of the conditions which are necessary for them. These conditions may be summarized as follows: (1) The great elevation of the region. (2) The horizontality of the strata. (3) A series of strata containing very massive beds, which differ greatly among themselves in respect to durability, but each member or subordinate group being quite homogeneous in all its horizontal extent; in a word, heterogeneity in vertical range and homogeneity in horizontal range. (4) An arid climate.

I. It is at once apparent that great elevation is essential to the production of high reliefs in the topography by the agency of erosion. Only in a high country can the streams corrade deeply, and it is by corrasion that the features of this region have been originated and blocked out. The elevation, however, is a condition whose immediate consequences are associated with corrasion, while it affects weathering only secondarily or remotely. The principal effect is the determination of the heights of the cliffs and the magnitudes of the topographical reliefs in general. All this seems so obvious that discussion is superfluous.

II. No less obvious is the effect of the horizontality of the strata. The long, flat crestlines, the constant profiles maintained for scores of miles along the edges of each stratigraphic series, would not be possible otherwise. . . .

III. The vertical heterogeneity is the character which gives complexity to the profile. Where the beds are numerous and where they differ among themselves as to durability, the profile becomes very complicated, like a very elaborate series of horizontal moldings.

IV. The effects of an arid climate are by no means simple nor intelligible at a glance. They appear only upon analysis, and the analysis must take cognizance of a wide range of facts. I cannot do better here than to have recourse to the excellent analysis of Gilbert:

All the processes of erosion are affected directly by the rainfall and by its distribution through the year. All are accelerated by its increase and retarded by its diminution. When it is concentrated in one part of the year at the expense of the remainder, transportation and corrasion are accelerated and weathering retarded. Weathering is favored by abundance of moisture. Frost accomplishes most when the rocks are saturated, and solution when there is the freest circulation. But when the annual rainfall is concentrated into a limited season, a large share of the water fails to penetrate and gain from temporary flooding does not compensate for the checking of all solution by a long, dry season.

Transportation is favored by increasing the water supply as greatly as by increasing declivity. When the volume of a stream increases it becomes at the same time more rapid, and its transporting capacity gains by the increment to velocity as well as by the increment to volume. Hence the increase in power of transportation is more than proportional to the increase of volume. It is due to this fact chiefly that the transportation of a stream which is subject to floods is greater than it would be if its total water supply were evenly distributed in time.

The indirect influence of rainfall and temperature by means of vegetation has different laws. Vegetation is intimately related to water supply. There is little or none where the annual precipitation is small, and it is profuse where the latter is great—especially when the temperature is at the same time high. In proportion as vegetation is profuse, the solvent power of percolating water is increased, and on the other hand the ground is sheltered from the mechanical action of rains and rills. The removal of disintegrated rock is greatly impeded by the conservative power of roots and fallen leaves, and a soil it thus preserved. Transportation is retarded. Weathering by solution is accelerated up to a certain point, but in the end it suffers by the clogging of transportation. The work of frost is nearly stopped as soon as the depth of soil exceeds the limit of frost action. The force of raindrops is expended on foliage. Moreover, a deep soil acts as a distributing reservoir for the water of rains and tends to equalize the flow of streams. Hence the general effect of vegetation is to retard erosion; and since the direct effect of great rainfall is the acceleration of erosion, it results that its direct and indirect tendencies are in opposite directions.

In arid regions of which the declivities are sufficient to give thorough drainage, the absence of vegetation is accompanied by absence of soil. When a shower falls, nearly all the water runs off from the bare rock, and the little that is absorbed is rapidly reduced by evaporation. Solution becomes a slow process for lack of a continuous supply of water, and frost accomplishes its work only when it closely follows the infrequent rain. Thus weathering is retarded. Transportation has its work concentrated by the quick gathering of showers into floods so as to compensate, in part at least, for the smallness of the total rainfall from which they derive their power.

In this analysis of Mr. Gilbert I fully concur. It remains only to apply the principles he has developed. The effects which he deduces from an arid climate in a high country are a scanty soil, a diminished rate of weathering, and a great efficiency of transportation. We must further consider the effects of these varied conditions upon a country composed of horizontal strata which are vertically heterogeneous. The paucity of soil lays bare the edges of the rocks. The gentler slopes or taluses being found in the softer beds, these are more readily weathered than they would be if the soil were more abundant. But harder beds are not so easily dissolved, and can be broken down only by the undermining resulting from the waste of underlying softer beds. Hence the hard strata form vertical ledges, while the softer beds form taluses or steep slopes, partially protected by debris and soil. In a word, the effect of an arid climate upon such a region as the Plateau Country is to increase the amount of bare rock, to sharpen the profiles and make them irregular, and to generate cliffs. To enforce this idea, let us imagine a moist climate returning to this region. The rate of weathering in the harder beds would be accelerated and the fragments and finer materials would increase the amount of soil lying upon the sloped edges of the softer beds, and the weathering of the latter would be retarded. Vegetation would start into life and conserve this soil by clogging transportation, and the profiles would gradually lose their abrupt angular character and become softened and rounded, like those of the Appalachians.

I resume the discussion by Gilbert:

The Formation and Functions of the Talus

Since the attack of erosion under the conditions prevailing in the Plateau Country is mainly directed against the edges of the horizontal strata, and since these strata vary among themselves in respect to hardness or durability, it follows that the different beds would, if the exposures were equal, weather at different rates. The softer beds would disintegrate rapidly and undermine the edges of harder beds overlying them. The harder beds being robbed of support, cleave off by the joints and the fragments fall. The fragmental material thus produced is not immediately carried away, but remains in part and forms a talus. This talus, however, is ultimately dissipated by solution, disintegration, and transportation, and the rate at which it is finally carried off is in the long run sensibly equal to the rate at which its material is supplied. It remains to consider the arrangement which this fragmental matter takes and its reaction upon the rate and mode of weathering. We may reach the matter most easily by discussing a hypothetical arbitrary case.

Let us suppose a series of strata consisting of four groups (see drawing), the uppermost group (A) being obdurate or very unyielding to the attack of weathering; the next below (B) being notably softer or less obdurate; the third (C) being hard; and the fourth (D) soft.* Conceive a stream corrading a gash nearly but not quite through the hard upper stratum. The

DEVELOPMENT OF CLIFF PROFILES

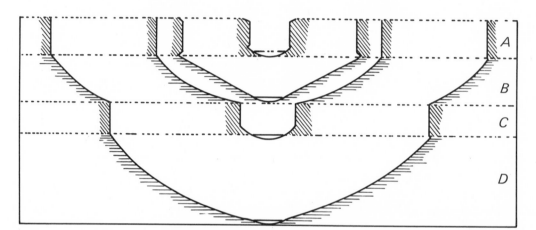

Development of Canyon Profile

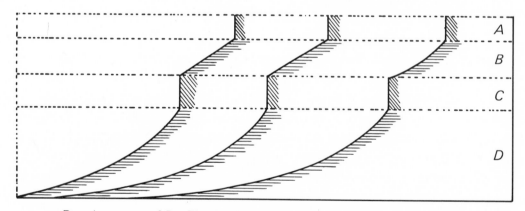

Development of Profiles by Recession—Upper and Lower Aubrey

*I am unable to think of a pair of adjectives which will suitably express the great and small degrees of obduracy of rocks against weathering. I shall use the terms "hard" and "soft," therefore, in this sense.

quantity of fragmental material furnished will vary (*ceteris paribus*) inversely with the hardness of the rock, and since the hardness is assumed to be great, the quantity supplied will be small. On the other hand, the fragments falling into the stream are quickly dissipated by corrasion. In other words, the removal of debris by transportation is for a time at the extreme of rapidity. Corrasion, moreover, while a country is rising, is a very rapid process in comparison with the rate of recession of a hard, massive wall. Very little talus, therefore, can form at this stage; the obduracy of the wall rock prevents its recession; little material is supplied which could serve to form a talus, and that little is quickly swept off by the stream. Hence the canyon will be narrow, with vertical or nearly vertical walls, and no appreciable talus will accumulate.

Conceive now the corrasion to go on until the stream has cut nearly but not quite through the soft group B. The supply of debris is greatly increased. The soft beds weather easily and undermine the hard beds above. Let us recall here that the width of the cut is no greater than the width of the water surface. As the cliff recedes the fragments begin to find a lodgment at its base, and though some of them roll into the stream and are devoured, yet another portion must await the slower process of solution and gradual decay before disappearing. Thus the rate of transportation slackens by the decreasing declivity of the river, while the rate of supply of debris increases. As the cliff further recedes the talus mounts higher and higher up the breast of the softer part of the wall. The faces of the softer strata become in due time a slope capable of supporting a talus.

Conceive now the stream cutting nearly but not quite through the second hard group C. The case here is not quite the same as when it was cut near to the base of A; for in the earlier or higher stage of the river all the debris came from A alone; while in the present case A, B, and C are all furnishing fragmental matter. Hence the corrasion is slackened and a small amount of talus may accumulate at the edge of the stream. Still the edges of C will be nearly vertical except very near the bottom.

Finally, conceive the stream to have cut through the soft group D, and suppose that at the bottom of this group it remains for a considerable period at a base level. The edges of D are steadily sapped and C is undermined. But the undermining of C cuts off the foot of the slope in B, increasing the declivity in that group and facilitating the descent of fragments. And this, in turn, accelerates the rate of weathering in B and the rate of undermining of A. Thus, curiously enough, the state of affairs at the bottom of the canyon influences the rate of recession at the summit of its wall.

We must now note the fact that a talus acts as a protecting mantle to the rocks it covers, screening them partially from dissolution by weathering. The heavier the talus the greater is the protection. But the amount of talus which can remain at any given level is dependent inversely upon the slope; and the talus is always descending by the action of the rains. Hence the accumulation is greatest at the bottom of the canyon. When, therefore, the recession of the wall has gone so far that the descending fragments do not fall at once into the stream, the lowest beds of all receive the most protection. The rate of recession of these lowest beds, therefore, becomes retarded. The protection diminishes as we go higher and the rate of recession increases correspondingly.

It follows at once that the talus is the regulator of the cliff profile; for it checks the rate of recession in the softer beds, keeping their recession *down* to the mean rate, while, by undermining, the recession of the hard beds is brought *up* to the mean rate. As soon as the talus is established on the lowest slope (D), the cliff may be said to have attained its normal profile, and in all subsequent recession that profile undergoes little change. The only modification it receives is a decrease in the slope D, which becomes longer and also takes the form of a curve, concave upward. The cause of this curvature is as follows. If the rate of recession in the soft beds, as due to the protection of talus, were proportional in a simple ratio to the height above the bottom, the slope would be straight, but would gradually decrease its inclination as the cliff recedes. But, in fact, the law governing the rate of recession is more complex. The protection given to the lower beds increases downwards in a higher ratio than a simple one, being as the square of the distance below the base of C, or, perhaps, in a still higher ratio. This arises from the fact that not only is the quantity of debris and soil greater in the lowest beds, but it is finer and more compact. Hence the rate of recession becomes inversely proportional to the square (?) of the distance below the base of C, and the curve becomes a segment of an hyperbola. . . .

In the foregoing discussion we have all the conditions necessary for understanding the cliff work and sculpture of the Grand Canyon, and we may now proceed to apply these principles to the peculiar profiles which the chasm presents in its several portions. The summit beds, consisting of arenaceous [sandy] and cherty [flintlike] limestones, are of medium obduracy. They contain a large amount of silicious matter, and if blocks of it were submitted to the stonecutter they would be pronounced excessively tough and hard; but, owing to the presence of an abundant calcareous cement of soluble character, it yields readily to weathering. Much of the silica has been aggregated into the form of cherty nodules, which are very abundant, forming, indeed, a considerable percentage of the entire mass of these beds. The nodules are to a considerable extent arranged in horizontal bands, occurring at frequent intervals, with separating layers of sandy limestone, in which the nodules, though still numerous, are less frequent. In the process of weathering, the nodules are less easily dissolved than the inclosing matrix, and as the rock decays they are left projecting from its mass, giving the faces at a little distance the appearance of a bedded conglomerate. Ultimately they are detached and fall down upon the talus below. Millions of these nodules are found in the great talus across the edges of the lower Aubrey.

The thickness of the upper Aubrey [Kaibab and Toroweap] limestones (of which there are several members of somewhat varied constitution) is altogether about 700 feet. Beneath them comes the hardest and most obdurate mass of the entire Carboniferous series—the cross-bedded [Coconino] sandstone. Its thickness is about 350 to 375 feet. It forms a vertical ledge which is seldom broken into a slope. It is seen as a most conspicuous band in the summit wall in every amphitheater and promontory. Beneath it is a vast mass of rather thinly bedded sandstones [hermit and Supai shales], constituting the lower Aubrey group. Their total thickness exceeds a thousand feet. These sandstones are the most yielding of any portion of the Carboniferous series, since the cement which holds the mass together is to a notable extent gypsiferous. It seldom forms a great cliff, but is in reality a succession of ledges often imperfect and beveled off, but sometimes well marked and precipitous. The individual ledges are of very small altitude, corresponding to the thickness of the several members. They are to a considerable degree protected by the nodules of chert and the slabs of hard sandstone shot down from the calcareous members and cross-bedded sandstone above. In the vast expanse of wall surface the individuality of the separate ledges disappears, and the general effect conveyed by the lower Aubrey is that of a long, steep, and regular slope. When seen in profile the true slope is readily appreciated; but when viewed directly in front, or with moderate obliquity, it looks too steep for human foothold, though it is by no means so. . . .

Let us endeavor to infer the typical forms of cliff profiles generated by the combined action of corrasion and weathering in the strata thus far described. Imagine first a stream corrading its channel through the upper Aubrey limestones. The degree of abruptness in the slopes descending to the stream would be dependent upon the rate of weathering relatively to the rate of corrasion. If the rate of corrasion were slow and the rate of weathering rapid the slopes would be gentle or at a low angle; if the corrasion were rapid and the weathering slow the banks would be precipitous. Imagine the stream to corrade still further into and through the very obdurate cross-bedded sandstone. Upon this latter rock, weathering has but little effect directly. It may stand for long geological periods with but a slight loss of substance, provided it is not undermined. Corrasion, however, may go on in it at a rate somewhat retarded by its obduracy indeed, but only a little less rapidly than in much softer rocks; for declivity and the amount of protection afforded by the clastic material in the bed of a stream are incomparably more potent factors than the hardness of the bedrock in determining the rate of corrasion. But the rate of weathering is dependent upon the nature of the stratum itself. Hence the limestones above would be much less precipitous than the adamantine sandstone below.

Imagine, further, the sinking of the channel deep into the very easily weathered shaly sandstones of the lower Aubrey. The problem now becomes a little more complicated. As before, the quality of the newly cut rocks does not necessarily imply any great increase in the rate of corrasion. But it does imply a modification in the rate of weathering and in the consequent form of the profile. A new factor now enters in the plan of operations. In consequence of their very yielding character the shaly sandstones are rapidly dissolved and the adamantine stratum above is *undermined.* The rate of recession becomes in the harder stratum equal to that in the softer shales beneath it. So rapid at first is this decay that at a certain early stage of the penetration of shales by the corrading stream the cross-bedded sandstone and the cherty limestones above often form a single ledge. The rate at which they are undermined is for a time greater than the rate of recession in the medium-hard cherty limestones. But this condition is gradually brought to a check by the formation of a talus. We have observed that the softer and more yielding the beds under the action of weathering the longer and less steep will be the weathered slope across their edges. Upon this slope across the edges of the shaly sandstones accumulate many of the cherty nodules and fragments of the adamantine sandstone, with large quantities of fine sand, and even a little soil. The debris lodging there protects, to an important extent, the shaly sandstones and retards more and more their rate of weathering, retards the rate of undermining, and diminishes gradually the supply of debris to the talus. Thus the great increase in the rate of weathering caused by corrasion penetrating the yielding shales is, to a great extent, countervailed by the formation of the talus. It now becomes apparent that the resulting profile of the entire cliff has a perfectly definite and stable configuration or typical form, which the combined action of all the incident forces tends strongly to maintain.

The cliff formed out of the upper and lower Aubrey series is very remarkable for the constancy of its profile throughout the entire extent of the great chasm. Along every mile of the main façade, in every amphitheater and alcove, and in every promontory, wing wall, and gable, it discloses the same familiar features. It is the wall of the upper or outer chasm. In the Kanab, Uinkaret, and Sheavwits divisions it stands far away from the lower or inner chasm—an interval of two miles usually separating its base from the brink of the inner gorge. In the Kaibab division the Aubrey wall is unchanged in its general character, but everything below it is there in strong contrast with what is disclosed in the other divisions. In the three western divisions the broad platform at the base of the upper wall is a very striking feature; in the Kaibab the platform is quarried away by the lower depths of the amphitheaters, leaving only intervening buttes, and the profile at the base of the great lower Aubrey talus at once plunges vertically down the precipices of the Red Wall limestone. In many places the Aubrey cliff in its recession by waste is so closely pursued by the recession of the Red Wall below that a few hundred feet of the lower Aubrey talus are cut off and the shales at the base of that series are undermined, forming cliffs which are continuous vertically with the great Red Wall precipice below. . . .

There are certain forms in the contours or ground plans of cliffs which claim attention. One of the most striking features in the vast maze of cliffwork in the Grand Canyon is found in the extremely tortuous lines of frontage. They wind about in a most intricate manner and rarely extend in straight lines through any considerable distances. The lines of trend usually are a succession of sweeping curves and sharp angles. The first view is extremely confusing, and under the influence of many causes of optical delusion prevailing in the landscape, it is very difficult to see anything but chaos—an utter absence of anything like system or arrangement. But patient study and analysis at length reveal many striking evidences of order. If we consider any one of the larger amphitheaters opening laterally into the main chasm, we shall note that it has many lateral amphitheaters opening into it of an inferior order of magnitude. . . . All of them are the result of corrasion and weathering. They illustrate the remarkable uniformity of the rate of weathering. The upper ends of the minor recesses are usually rounded in contour. The longitudinal wall extending to its confluence with the main amphitheater makes at that point a sharp angle. The weathering of these walls has obviously originated in the corrading channels of the lateral tributaries and their minuter branches. As the narrow cleft cut by the sinking stream deepened it also widened. If we represent the locus of the edge of any stratum high in the series at successive epochs of the development by parallel equidistant lines, we shall have a series of curves running up the stream nearly parallel to its course, then circling around its head and returning to its mouth. As these curves recede from the stream the more nearly do they approach to arcs of circles. The same recession is going on in the walls of the main amphitheater, into which the minor one opens. Where two minor or major amphitheaters are situated near each other the recession of their walls at length obliterates a portion of the summit stratum which divided them, and at later stages successively obliterates lower and lower members. The great cloister buttes are formed by the recession of the walls of any two parallel major amphitheaters, and the wings of these buttes by the recession of the walls of the minor amphitheaters. The minor recesses exhibit the rounded contours at their upper ends. Everywhere is disclosed an approximate uniformity in the rate of recession. Where the expanding curves of recession from any two adjoining recesses meet or intersect, the included mass between them is carved sometimes into a cusp or sharp "spur," sometimes into a stately gable, according to the relative positions of the axes of the curves. The spurs are frequently very narrow and sharp, and in an advanced state of erosion such a spur in the Red Wall band breaks into a row of needles or pinnacles. Many of the gables are of most noble form and of wonderful symmetry. Human conception cannot surpass their beauty even if it can rival it.

The cusp contour is also repeated on a minor scale in the wall faces, where it appears as a minor decoration or fretting of the edges of the strata. It is especially conspicuous in the Kaibab. It appears to have its origin in minor corrasion by storm sluices, which at first scour out at frequent and regular intervals deep notches, which widen out by weathering, and once started the recesses or alcoves thus opened perpetuate themselves. The contour line along the face of the cliff thus curves inward and the intersection of two curves at their ends forms the cusp.

In the faces of the great limestone member of the Red Wall may be seen large niches or panels of very regular form spanned by circular arches above. . . . Sometimes they are very deeply recessed in the façade, sometimes only slightly so. There are literally hundreds of these niches along the extent of the limestone front, and, so far as known, they are seen in no other member. . . .

Camping Accommodations in the National Parks

ACADIA NATIONAL PARK

Blackwoods (5 miles south of Bar Harbor)
Seawall (5 miles south of Southwest Harbor)

ARCHES NATIONAL PARK

Devil's Garden (18 miles north of Visitor Center)

BIG BEND NATIONAL PARK

Castolon Cottonwood (36 miles southwest of
  Headquarters)
Chisos Mountains Lower Basin (10 miles southwest of
  Headquarters)
Panther Junction Trailer Court (Park Headquarters)
Rio Grande Trailer Village
Rio Grande Village (20 miles southeast of Headquarters)

BRYCE CANYON NATIONAL PARK

North (at Headquarters)
Sunset (1 mile south of Headquarters)

CANYONLANDS NATIONAL PARK

Squaw Flat (38 miles west of U.S. 160)

CAPITOL REEF NATIONAL PARK

Capitol Reef ($1\frac{1}{4}$ miles south of Utah 24)

CRATER LAKE NATIONAL PARK

Lost Creek (on Pinnacles Road)
Mazama (0.3 mile east of Annie Springs Entrance)
Rim (Rim Village)

EVERGLADES NATIONAL PARK

Broad River (back country)
Cane Patch (back country)
Camp Lonesome (back country)
Chickees (various locations)
Crocodile Point (back country)
Flamingo (38 miles south of Entrance)
Graveyard Creek (back country)
Hell's Bay (back country)
Indian Key (back country)
Little Rabbit Key (back country)
Long Pine Key (5 miles south of Entrance)
Lopez River (back country)
Lostman's River (back country)
New Turkey Key (back country)
North Nest Key (back country)
Onion Key (back country)
Rabbit Key (back country)

Sandy Key (back country)
South Lostman's River (back country)
Watson Place (back country)
Wedge Point (back country)
Willy Willy (back country)

GLACIER NATIONAL PARK

Apgar (2 miles north of West Entrance)
Avalanche (16 miles northeast of West Entrance)
Bowman Creek (¼ mile north of Poleridge Entrance)
Bowman Lake (6 miles east of Poleridge Entrance)
Cut Bank (4 miles west of U.S. 89)
Fish Creek (4 miles northwest of West Entrance)
Kintla Lake (15 miles north of Poleridge Entrance)
Logging Creek (14 miles south of Poleridge Entrance)
Many Glacier (13 miles west of Babb)
Quartz Creek (8 miles south of Poleridge Entrance)
Rising Sun (6 miles west of St. Mary Entrance)
River (North Fork) (2 miles north of Poleridge Entrance)
Sprague Creek (9 miles north of West Entrance)
St. Mary Lake (1 mile northwest of St. Mary Entrance)
Two Medicine (7 miles west of Montana 49)
Back-country Camps (70 in park)

GRAND CANYON NATIONAL PARK

North Rim (13 miles south of North Entrance)
Desert View (½ mile west of East Entrance)
Mather (Grand Canyon Village)
Trailer Village (Grand Canyon Village)

HIKE-IN CAMPGROUNDS

Bright Angel Creek (Phantom Ranch)
Cottonwood (North Kaibab Trail)
Havasu (Havasu Canyon)
Indian Gardens (Bright Angel Trail)
Roaring Springs (North Kaibab Trail)

GRAND TETON NATIONAL PARK

Colter Bay (9 miles northwest of Moran)
Colter Bay Trailer Village (9 miles northwest of Moran)

Gros Ventre (10 miles southeast of Moose)
Jenny Lake (7 miles north of Moose)
Lizard Creek (17 miles northwest of Moran)
Signal Mountain (7 miles southwest of Moran)

GREAT SMOKY MOUNTAINS NATIONAL PARK

Abrams Creek (31 miles south of Maryville, Tennessee)
Balsam Mountain
Big Creek (1 mile west of Mount Sterling, North Carolina)
Cades Cove (10 miles southwest of Townsend, Tennessee)
Cataloochee (20 miles northwest of Waynesville, North Carolina)
Cosby (7 miles south of Cosby, Tennessee)
Deep Creek (2 miles north of Bryson City, North Carolina)
Elkmont (8 miles west of Gatlinburg)
Look Rock (11 miles southwest of Walland, Tennessee)
Smokemont (6 miles north of Cherokee, North Carolina)
Trail Shelters (along Appalachian Trail)
Miscellaneous Camps (95 throughout the park)

GUADALUPE MOUNTAINS NATIONAL PARK

Pine Springs Canyon

HALEAKALA NATIONAL PARK

Holua (near Holua Cabin)
Hosmer Grove (½ mile east of North Entrance)
Kipohulu (near Seven Pools)
Paliku (near Paliku Cabin)

HAWAII VOLCANOES NATIONAL PARK

Kamoamoa (52 miles southwest of Park Headquarters)
Kipuka Nene (12 miles south of Park Headquarters)
Namakani Paio (3 miles west of Park Headquarters)

HOT SPRINGS NATIONAL PARK

Gulpha Gorge (2 miles east of Hot Springs)

ISLE ROYALE NATIONAL PARK

Beaver Island (Washington Harbor)
Belle Isle (North Side)
Birch Island (North Side)
Caribou Island (Rock Harbor)
Chickenbone Lake (Inland)
Chippewa Harbor (South Side)
Daisy Farm (Rock Harbor)
Duncan Bay (North Side)
Duncan Narrows (North Side)
East Chickenbone Lake (Inland)
Feltman Lake (Inland)
Grace Island (Grace Harbor)
Hatchet Lake (Inland)
Hay Bay (South Side)
Hugginin Cove (Northwest End)
Island Mine (Inland)
Lake Desor (Inland)
Lake Richie (Inland)
Lane Cove (Inland)
Little Todd Harbor (Inland)
McCargo Cove (North Side)
Malone Bay (South Side)
Merritt Lane (Northeast End)
Moskey Basin (Rock Harbor)
North Lake Desor (Inland)
Rock Harbor (Rock Harbor)
Siskiwit Bay (South Side)
South Lake Desor (Inland)
Three-mile (Rock Harbor)
Todd Harbor (North Side)
Tookers Island (Rock Harbor)
Washington Creek (Washington Harbor)

KINGS CANYON NATIONAL PARK

Azalea (½ mile north of Grant Grove)
Canyon View (31 miles northeast of Grant Grove)
Crystal Springs (½ mile north of Grant Grove)

Moraine (32 miles northeast of Grant Grove)
Sentinel (30 miles northeast of Grant Grove)
Sheep Creek (29 miles northeast of Grant Grove)
Sunset (½ mile south of Grant Grove)
Swale (1 mile northwest of Grant Grove)

LASSEN VOLCANIC NATIONAL PARK

Butte Lake (northeast corner of park)
Crags (48 miles east of Redding)
Juniper Lake (13 miles north of Chester)
Lost Creek (5 miles east of Manzanita Lake)
Sulphur Works (southwest Entrance)
Summit Lake (12 miles south of Manzanita Lake)
Warner Valley (16 miles northwest of Chester)

MAMMOTH CAVE NATIONAL PARK

Headquarters
Houchin's Ferry (2 miles northeast of Brownsville)

MESA VERDE NATIONAL PARK

Morfield Canyon (5 miles south of Entrance)

MOUNT McKINLEY NATIONAL PARK

Igloo (mile 33)
Morino (mile .05)
Riley Creek (mile 0.1)
Sanctuary (mile 22)
Savage (mile 12)
Teklanika (mile 29)
Wonder Lake (mile 84)

MOUNT RAINIER NATIONAL PARK

Cougar Rock (8 miles northeast of Nisqually Entrance)
Ipsut Creek (5 miles east of Carbon River Entrance)
Longmire (6 miles northeast of Nisqually Entrance)
Ohanapecosh (1½ miles south of Stevens Canyon Entrance)
Sunrise (15 miles west of White River Entrance)
Sunshine Point (⅕ mile east of Nisqually Entrance)
White River (5 miles west of White River Entrance)

NORTH CASCADES NATIONAL PARK

Stehekin Valley Campgrounds (distance from Stehekin)
Bridge Creek (16 miles)
Cottonwood (23 miles)
Dolly Varden (14 miles)
High Bridge (11 miles)
Shady (15 miles)
Tumwater (13 miles)

OLYMPIC NATIONAL PARK

Altaire (12 miles west of Port Angeles)
Boulder Creek (8 miles west of Port Angeles)
Deer Park (22 miles southeast of Port Angeles)
Dosewallips (15 miles west of Brinnon)
Elwha (10 miles west of Port Angeles)
Erickson Bay (west shore of Ozette Lake)
Fairholm (26 miles west of Port Angeles)
Graves Creek (20 miles east of Amanda Park)
Heart O' The Hills (5½ miles south of Port Angeles)
Hoh (22 miles southeast of Forks)
July Creek (6 miles northeast of Amanda Park)
Kalaloch (35 miles south of Forks)
Mora (15 miles west of Forks)
North Fork Quinault (20 miles northeast of Amanda Park)
Queets (25 miles southeast of Queets)
Soleduck (40 miles southwest of Port Angeles)
Staircase (19 miles northwest of Hoodsport)

PLATT NATIONAL PARK

Central (½ mile east of North Entrance)
Cold Springs (1 mile east of North Entrance)
Rock Creek (1½ miles west of North Entrance)

ROCKY MOUNTAIN NATIONAL PARK

Aspenglen (at Fall River Entrance)
Glacier Basin (5 miles on Bear Lake Road)
Longs Peak (11 miles south of Estes Park)
Moraine Park (2 miles on Bear Lake Road)
Timber Creek (11 miles north of Grand Lake)
Trail Camps (throughout park)

SEQUOIA NATIONAL PARK

Atwell Mill (20 miles east of Hammond)
Buckeye Flat (5 miles north of Headquarters)
Dorst 1–4 (28 miles north of Headquarters)
Lodgepole (21 miles north of Headquarters)
Potwisha (3 miles north of Headquarters)
South Fork (15 miles south of Three Rivers)

SHENANDOAH NATIONAL PARK

Milepost
22.2 Matthews Arm
51.2 Big Meadows
57.5 Lewis Mountain
79.5 Loft Mountain
83.7 Dundo Group Campground

VIRGIN ISLANDS NATIONAL PARK

Cinnamon Bay

VOYAGEURS NATIONAL PARK

King William
Mukooda

WIND CAVE NATIONAL PARK

Elk Mountain (1 mile north of Headquarters)

YELLOWSTONE NATIONAL PARK

Bridge Bay (3 miles southwest of Lake Junction)
Canyon (¼ mile east of Canyon Junction)
Fishing Bridge (1 mile east of Lake Junction)
Fishing Bridge Trailer Court (1½ miles east of Lake Junction)

Grant Village (2 miles south of West Thumb Junction)
Indian Creek (7 miles south of Mammoth)
Lewis Lake (10 miles south of West Thumb)
Madison ($\frac{1}{4}$ mile west of Madison Junction)
Mammoth ($\frac{1}{2}$ mile north of Mammoth)
Norris (1 mile north of Norris Junction)
Pebble Creek (7 miles southwest of Northeast Entrance)
Slough Creek (10 miles east of Tower Fall Junction)
Tower Fall (3 miles east of Tower Junction)

YOSEMITE NATIONAL PARK

(Camp 4 Yosemite Valley) Sunnyside
(Camp 7 Yosemite Valley) Lower River
(Camp 9 Yosemite Valley) Youth Group
(Camp 11 Yosemite Valley) Upper Pines
(Camp 12 Yosemite Valley) North Pines
(Camp 14 Yosemite Valley) Lower Pines
(Camp 15 Yosemite Valley) Upper River

Bridalveil Creek (24 miles from Yosemite Valley)
Crane Flat (9 miles south of Big Oak Flat Entrance)
Harden Lake (1$\frac{1}{2}$ miles north of White Wolf)
Hodgdon Meadow ($\frac{1}{2}$ mile south of Big Oak Flat)
Porcupine Creek (6 miles west of Tenaya Lake)
Porcupine Flat (6 miles west of Tenaya Lake)
Smoky Jack (10 miles east of Crane Flat)
Soda Springs (4.5 miles west of Tioga Pass)
Tamarack Flat (5 miles southeast of Crane Flat)
Tenaya Lake (8 miles west of Tioga Pass)
Tuolumne Meadows (4 miles west of Tioga Pass)
Wawona (6 miles north of South Entrance)
White Wolf (25 miles west of Tioga Pass)
Yosemite Creek (17 miles west of Tioga Pass)

ZION NATIONAL PARK

Lava Point
South (at South Entrance)
Watchman (at South Entrance)

APPENDIX C

Addresses of the National Parks

Prospective national park visitors should obtain advance information about camping areas, fishing and boating regulations, accesses, accommodations, etc. They can write to the superintendents of the respective parks at the addresses listed below or consult *Camping in the National Park System*, available through the Superintendent of Documents, U. S. Government Printing Office, Washington, D.C. 20402.

ACADIA NATIONAL PARK
Route 1, Box 1
Bar Harbor, Maine 04609

ARCHES NATIONAL PARK
c/o Canyonlands National Park
Moab, Utah 84532

BIG BEND NATIONAL PARK
Big Bend National Park, Texas 79834

BRYCE CANYON NATIONAL PARK
Bryce Canyon, Utah 84717

CANYONLANDS NATIONAL PARK
Moab, Utah 84532

CAPITOL REEF NATIONAL PARK
Torrey, Utah 84775

CRATER LAKE NATIONAL PARK
Box 7
Crater Lake, Oregon 97604

EVERGLADES NATIONAL PARK
Box 279
Homestead, Florida 33030

GLACIER NATIONAL PARK
West Glacier, Montana 59936

GRAND CANYON NATIONAL PARK
Box 129
Grand Canyon, Arizona 86023

GRAND TETON NATIONAL PARK
Box 67
Moose, Wyoming 83012

GREAT SMOKY MOUNTAINS NATIONAL PARK
Gatlinburg, Tennessee 37738

GUADALUPE MOUNTAINS NATIONAL PARK
c/o Carlsbad Caverns National Park
3225 National Parks Highway
Carlsbad, New Mexico 88220

HALEAKALA NATIONAL PARK
Box 537
Makawau, Maui, Hawaii 96768

HAWAII VOLCANOES NATIONAL PARK
Hawaii Volcanoes National Park

Hawaii 96718

HOT SPRINGS NATIONAL PARK
Box 1219
Hot Springs National Park, Arkansas 71901

ISLE ROYALE NATIONAL PARK
87 North Ripley Street
Houghton, Michigan 49931

KINGS CANYON NATIONAL PARK
Three Rivers, California 93271

LASSEN VOLCANIC NATIONAL PARK
Mineral, California 96063

MAMMOTH CAVE NATIONAL PARK
Mammoth Cave, Kentucky 42259

MESA VERDE NATIONAL PARK
Mesa Verde National Park, Colorado 81330

MOUNT McKINLEY NATIONAL PARK
McKinley Park, Alaska 99755

MOUNT RAINIER NATIONAL PARK
Longmire, Washington 98397

NORTH CASCADES NATIONAL PARK
Sedro Woolley, Washington 98284

OLYMPIC NATIONAL PARK
600 East Park Avenue
Port Angeles, Washington 98362

PLATT NATIONAL PARK
Box 201
Sulphur, Oklahoma 73086

ROCKY MOUNTAIN NATIONAL PARK
Estes Park, Colorado 80517

SEQUOIA NATIONAL PARK
Three Rivers, California 93271

SHENANDOAH NATIONAL PARK
Luray, Virginia 22835

VIRGIN ISLANDS NATIONAL PARK
Cinnamon Bay Camp, P.O. Box 4930
St. Thomas, U.S. Virgin Islands 00801

VOYAGEURS NATIONAL PARK
International Falls, Minnesota 56649

WIND CAVE NATIONAL PARK
Hot Springs, South Dakota 57747

YELLOWSTONE NATIONAL PARK
Yellowstone National Park, Wyoming 82190

YOSEMITE NATIONAL PARK
Box 577 (Yosemite Village)
Yosemite National Park, California 95389

ZION NATIONAL PARK
Springdale, Utah 84767

Camping Accommodations and Addresses of the National Monuments

BADLANDS NATIONAL MONUMENT

Box 72, Interior, South Dakota 57750
    Cedar Pass (5 miles southwest of Northeast
      Entrance)
    Sage Creek Primitive (11 miles west of Pinnacles
      Entrance)

BANDELIER NATIONAL MONUMENT

Los Alamos, New Mexico 87544
    Juniper ($\frac{1}{10}$ mile inside Entrance)
    Ponderosa (6 miles west of Entrance)

BISCAYNE NATIONAL MONUMENT

P.O. Box 1369, Homestead, Florida 33030
    Elliott Key (8 miles east of Homestead Bayfront
      Park)

BLACK CANYON OF THE GUNNISON NATIONAL MONUMENT

c/o General Superintendent, Curecanti Group,
P.O. Box 1648, Montrose, Colorado 81401
    North Rim (11 miles southwest of Colorado 92)
    South Rim (6 miles north of U.S. 50)

CANYON DE CHELLY NATIONAL MONUMENT

Box 588, Chinle, Arizona 86503
    Cottonwood (1 mile east of Entrance)

CHACO CANYON NATIONAL MONUMENT

Star Route, Bloomfield, New Mexico 87413
    Gallo Wash (1 mile east of Visitor Center)

CHANNEL ISLANDS NATIONAL MONUMENT

1699 Anchors Way Drive, Ventura, California 93003
    Anacapa Island (13 miles south of Channel Island
      Harbor)
    Santa Barbara Island (38 miles southwest of
      Headquarters)

CHIRICAHUA NATIONAL MONUMENT

Dos Cabezas Star Route
Willcox, Arizona 86543
    Bonita Canyon ($\frac{1}{2}$ mile east of Head Quarters)

COLORADO NATIONAL MONUMENT

Fruita, Colorado 81521
    Saddle Horn (3 miles south of West Entrance)

CRATERS OF THE MOON NATIONAL MONUMENT

Box 29, Arco, Idaho 83213
    Lava Flow (Headquarters)

DEATH VALLEY NATIONAL MONUMENT

Death Valley, California 92328
    Furnace Creek (north of visitor center)
    Mahogany Flat (9 miles southeast of Wildrose
      Ranger Station)
    Mesquite Springs (5 miles south of Scotty's Castle)
    Stove Pipe Wells
    Sunset (opposite visitor center)
    Texas Springs ($\frac{1}{2}$ mile east of Furnace Creek)
    Thorndike (8 miles southeast of Wildrose Ranger
      Station)
    Wildrose ($\frac{1}{8}$ mile west of Wildrose Ranger Station)

DEVILS POSTPILE NATIONAL MONUMENT

c/o Sequoia & Kings Canyon National Parks
Three Rivers, California 93271

DEVILS TOWER NATIONAL MONUMENT

Devils Tower, Wyoming 82714
    Belle Fourche River (1 mile inside Entrance)

DINOSAUR NATIONAL MONUMENT

Box 210, Dinosaur, Colorado 81610
    Anderson Hole (Yampa Canyon)
    Box Elder (Yampa Canyon)
    Deerlodge Park (16 miles northwest of Elk Springs)
    Echo Park (38 miles north and east of Dinosaur)
    Gates of Lodore (49 miles east of visitor center)
    Harding Hole (Yampa Canyon)
    Jones Hole (Whirlpool Canyon)
    Lower Wade & Curtis (Lodore Canyon)
    Pot Creek (Lodore Canyon)
    Rainbow Park (Green River)
    Rippling Brook (Lodore Canyon)
    Split Mountain (4 miles east of visitor center)

    Tepee Hole (Yampa Canyon)
    Triplet Falls (Lodore Canyon)
    Warm Springs (Yampa Canyon)

EL MORRO NATIONAL MONUMENT

Ramah, New Mexico 87321
    El Morro ($\frac{1}{2}$ mile from Headquarters)

FORT JEFFERSON NATIONAL MONUMENT

c/o Everglades National Park
Box 279, Homestead, Florida 33030
    No Camping Accommodations

GLACIER BAY NATIONAL MONUMENT

Gustavus, Alaska 99826
    Wilderness Camping (throughout area)

GRAND CANYON NATIONAL MONUMENT

c/o Grand Canyon National Park
Box 129, Grand Canyon, Arizona 86023
    Monument (Toroweap Point)

GREAT SAND DUNES NATIONAL MONUMENT

Box 60, Alamosa, Colorado 81101
    Dunes (1 mile northwest of Headquarters)
    Pinyon Flats (1 mile north of Headquarters)

HOVENWEEP NATIONAL MONUMENT

c/o Mesa Verde National Park
Mesa Verde National Park, Colorado 81330
    Square Tower Ruin (26 miles southwest of
      Pleasantview)

JOSHUA TREE NATIONAL MONUMENT

74458 Palm Vista Drive
Twentynine Palms, California 92277
    Belle (11 miles south of Twentynine Palms)
    Cottonwood Spring (30 miles east of Indio)
    Hidden Valley (14 miles south of Joshua Tree)
    Indian Cove (10 miles west of Twentynine Palms)
    Jumbo Rocks (14 miles south of Twentynine Palms)
    Ryan (16 miles south of Joshua Tree)
    Sheep Pass (18 miles south of Joshua Tree)
    White Tank ($12\frac{1}{2}$ miles south of Twentynine Palms)

KATMAI NATIONAL MONUMENT

Box 7, King Salmon, Alaska 99613
    Katmai Camping Area

LAVA BEDS NATIONAL MONUMENT

Box 867, Tulelake, California 96134
    Indian Well (Headquarters)

NATURAL BRIDGES NATIONAL MONUMENT

c/o Canyonlands National Park
Moab, Utah 84532
    Natural Bridges (4 miles off Utah 95)

NAVAJO NATIONAL MONUMENT

Tonalea, Arizona 86044
    No Camping Accommodations

ORGAN PIPE CACTUS NATIONAL MONUMENT

Box 38, Ajo, Arizona 85321
    Headquarters ($1\frac{1}{2}$ miles southwest of visitor center)

PINNACLES NATIONAL MONUMENT

Paicines, California 95043
    Chalone Annex (1 mile northwest of East Entrance)
    Chalone Creek (1 mile northwest of East Entrance)
    Chaparral (2 miles east of West Entrance)

APPENDIX E

Glossary of Geologist's and Naturalist's Terms*

AA—Hawaiian term for rough, clinkery lava. (Pronounced *ah-ah*.)

ABRASION—The wearing away of rocks by rubbing or grinding, chiefly by small grains of silt and sand carried by water or air currents and by glaciers.

AGATE—A variety of chalcedony with alternate layers of opal.

ALGAE—Simple forms of plants, most of which grow in water. Seaweeds are the most common forms found as fossils.

ALLUVIAL PLAIN—A plain formed by the deposition of materials from rivers and streams.

ALPINE GLACIER—A glacier confined to a stream valley; usually fed from a cirque. Also called valley glacier or mountain glacier.

AMPHIBIAN—A cold-blooded animal that breathes with gills in early stages of life and with lungs in later stages. Intermediate between fish and reptiles.

AMYGDALOID—A general name for volcanic rocks that contain numerous gas cavities (vesicles) filled with secondary minerals.

ANTICLINE—An arch, or upfold, of rock strata, with the flanks dipping in opposite directions from its axis.

ANTICLINORIUM—A series of anticlines and syn-

clines so arranged structurally that together they form a general arch or anticline.

APPALACHIAN REVOLUTION—The closing event of the Paleozoic Era; the time when the Appalachian Mountains were originally formed by buckling and folding.

AQUIFER—Porous, permeable, water-bearing layer of rock, sand, or gravel capable of supplying water to wells or springs.

ARCHEOZOIC—The earliest era of geologic time, during which the first known rocks were formed; known also as the Early Precambrian.

ARÊTE—Sharp crest of a mountain ridge between two cirques or two glaciated valleys.

ARTIFACTS—Structures or implements made by man.

ASH—Fine-grained material ejected from a volcano.

BASALT—A common extrusive igneous rock, usually occurring as lava flows and typically black or dark gray in color.

BASE LEVEL—The lowest level to which land can be eroded by running water; equivalent to sea level for the continents as a whole.

BASIN—Applied to a basin-shaped feature which may be either structural, with rocks dipping inwards, or purely topographical.

BATHOLITH—A huge mass of crystalline igneous rock originating within the earth's crust and extending to great depths.

BED—The smallest division of a stratified rock series.

*Glossary of Geologist's and Naturalist's Terms (slightly expanded by Milton Goldstein) from *A Guide to the National Parks* by William H. Matthews, III. Copyright © 1968, 1973 by William H. Matthews, III. Used by permission of Doubleday & Company, Inc.

BED LOAD—Material in movement along a stream bottom or, if wind is the transporting agency, along the surface.

BEDDING PLANES—Surfaces along which rock layers part readily, by which one layer may be distinguished from another.

BEDROCK—The unweathered solid rock of the earth's crust.

BERGSCHRUND—The gap between glacier ice and the headwall of a cirque.

BIOCHEMICAL ROCK—A sedimentary rock composed of deposits resulting directly or indirectly from the life processes of organisms.

BLOCK MOUNTAINS—Mountains that result from faulting.

BLUE RIDGE—The easternmost range of the Appalachian Mountain System, composed largely of very ancient Archeozoic and Proterozoic rocks.

BOMB, VOLCANIC—A mass of lava ejected from a volcanic vent in a plastic condition and then shaped in flight or as it hits the ground. Larger than one and a half inches across.

BOULDER—Large, water-worn, and rounded blocks of stone, most commonly found in stream beds, on beaches, or in glaciated areas.

BRAIDED STREAM—A stream whose channel is filled with deposits that split it into many small channels.

BREAKER—A wave breaking into foam in the shallow water near the shore.

BRECCIA—A rock made up of coarse, angular fragments of pre-existing rock that has been broken and the pieces recemented together.

BUTTE—A flat-topped, steep-walled hill; usually a remnant of horizontal beds, and smaller and narrower than a mesa.

CALCAREOUS—Composed of calcium carbonate.

CALCAREOUS ALGAE—Algae that form deposits of calcium carbonate, fossils of which are found in the United States.

CALCITE—A mineral composed of calcium carbonate, $CaCO_3$.

CALDERA—A large, basin-shaped volcanic depression.

CAMBRIAN—The earliest period of the Paleozoic Era or the system of rocks formed in this period.

CARBONIFEROUS—Composed largely of carbon. Also, a former period of the Paleozoic Era, now divided into the Mississippian and Pennsylvanian periods, so called because it contained the world's greatest coal deposits.

CEMENTATION—The process whereby loose grains, such as silt, sand, or gravels, are bound together by precipitation of mineral matter between them to produce firm rock beds.

CENOZOIC—The latest of geologic time, containing the Tertiary and Quaternary periods and continuing to the present time.

CENTRAL VENT—An opening in the earth's crust, roughly circular, from which magmatic products are extruded. A volcano is an accumulation of igneous material around a central vent.

CHALCEDONY—The noncrystalline forms of quartz, such as chert, flint, and agate.

CHEMICAL WEATHERING—The weathering of rock material by chemical processes whereby the original material is transformed into new chemical combinations.

CINDER CONE—Cone formed by the explosive type of volcanic eruption; it has a narrow base and steep, symmetrical slopes of interlocking, angular cinders.

CINDER, VOLCANIC—A fragment of lava, generally less than an inch in diameter, ejected from a volcanic vent.

CIRQUE—Steep-walled basin high on a mountain, produced by glacial erosion and commonly forming the head of a valley.

CLASTIC ROCK—Those rocks composed largely of fragments derived from pre-existing rocks and transported mechanically to their place of deposition, such as shales, siltstones, sandstones, and conglomerates.

CLASTIC TEXTURE—Texture shown by sedimentary rocks formed from deposits of mineral and rock fragments. *See* Clastic Rock.

CLAY—The finest type of soil or clastic fragments; having high plasticity when wet, and consisting mainly of aluminum and silica.

COAL—A black, compact sedimentary rock, containing 60 to 100 per cent of organic material, primarily of plant origin.

COASTAL PLAIN—An exposed part of the sea floor, normally consisting of stream- or wave-deposited sediments.

COL—A pass through a mountain ridge. Formed by the enlargement of two cirques on opposite sides of the ridge until their headwalls meet and are broken down.

COLUMN—A column or post of dripstone joining the floor and roof of a cave; the result of joining of a stalactite and a stalagmite.

COLUMNAR JOINTING—A pattern of jointing that blocks out columns of rock. Characteristic of tabular basalt flows or sills.

COMPLEX MOUNTAINS—Mountains that result from a combination of faulting, folding, and volcanic action.

COMPOSITE CONE—Cone formed by intermediate type of volcanic eruption, consisting of alternate layers of cinders and lava; also called a strato-volcano.

CONCHOIDAL—A characteristic break or fracture of a mineral or rock resulting in a smooth, curved surface. Typical of glass, quartz, and obsidian.

CONCORDANT PLUTON—An intrusive igneous body with contacts parallel to the layering or foliation surfaces of the rocks into which it was intruded.

CONCRETION—A nodular or irregularly shaped structure that has grown by mineral concentration around a nucleus, such as siderite concretions or oölitic hematite.

CONGLOMERATE—Water-worn pebbles cemented together; the pebbles are usually of mixed sizes.

CONTINENTAL GLACIER—An ice sheet that obscures mountains and plains of a large section of a continent. Existing continental glaciers are on Greenland and Antarctica.

CONTACT METAMORPHISM—Alteration of rocks caused by contact with igneous intrusions.

CONTINENTAL SHELF—The relatively shallow ocean floor bordering a continental landmass.

CONTOUR LINES—Lines of a map joining points on the earth having the same elevation.

COQUINA—A coarse-grained, porous variety of clastic limestone composed mostly of fragments of shells.

CORRASION—The scouring action of sand borne by wind and water.

CORRELATION—The process of establishing the contemporaneity of rocks or events in another area.

CRATER—A bowl-shaped depression, generally in the top of a volcanic cone.

CREEP—The slow, imperceptible movement of soil or broken rock from higher to lower levels.

CRETACEOUS—The latest period of the Mesozoic Era of geologic time.

CREVASSE—A deep crack in a glacier.

CRUST—The outer zone of the earth, composed of solid rock between twenty and thirty miles thick. Rests on the mantle, and may be covered by sediments.

CRYSTAL—The form of a mineral occurring in a geometric shape with flat or smooth faces meeting each other in definite angles.

CRYSTALLINE—Pertaining to the nature of a crystal, such as a rock composed of crystals or crystal grains; often glassy in appearance.

DECOMPOSITION—Term synonymous with chemical weathering.

DEFLATION—The removal of material from a land surface by wind action.

DEFORMATION—The result of diastrophism as shown in the tilting, bending, or breaking of layers of rock.

DELTA—A deposit of sediment built at the mouth of a stream as it enters a larger, quieter body of water, such as the sea, a lake, or sometimes a larger, more slowly flowing stream.

DEPOSITION—The laying down of material that may later become a rock or mineral deposit.

DETRITAL SEDIMENTARY ROCKS—Rocks formed from accumulations of minerals and rocks derived either from erosion of previously existing rocks or from the weathered products of these rocks.

DEVONIAN—The fourth period of the Paleozoic Era.

DIASTROPHISM—The process by which the earth's crust is deformed, producing folds and faults, rising or sinking of the lands and sea bottom, and the building of mountains.

DIFFERENTIAL WEATHERING—The process by which different sections of a rock mass weather at different rates. Caused primarily by variations in composition of the rock itself and also by differences in intensity of weathering from one section to another in the same rock.

DIKE—Wall of intrusive igneous rock cutting across the structure of other rocks.

DIORITE—A coarse-grained igneous rock with the composition of andesite (no quartz or orthoclase), composed of about 75 per cent plagioclase feldspars and the balance ferromagnesian silicates.

DIP—The slope of a bed of rock relative to the horizontal.

DISINTEGRATION—Synonymous with mechanical weathering.

DISTURBANCE—Regional mountain-building event in earth history, commonly separating two periods.

DIVIDE—The ridges or regions of high ground that separate the drainage basins of streams.

DOME—An upfolded area from which the rocks dip outward in all directions.

DRAINAGE BASIN—The area from which a given stream and its tributaries receive their water.

DRIFT—General term for glacial deposits.

DRIPSTONE—A deposit, usually of limestone, made by dripping water, such as stalactites and stalagmites in caverns.

DRUMLIN—Oval hill composed of glacial drift, with its long axis parallel to the direction of movement of a former ice sheet.

DUNE—A mound or ridge of wind-deposited sand.

EARTHQUAKE—The shaking of the ground as a result of movements within the earth, most commonly associated with movement along faults.

END MORAINE—A ridge or belt of till marking the farthest advance of a glacier; also called a terminal moraine.

ENVIRONMENT—Everything around a plant or animal that may affect it.

EOCENE—Second oldest epoch of the Tertiary Period of the Cenozoic Era.

EOLIAN—Pertaining to the erosion and the deposits resulting from wind action and to sedimentary rocks composed of wind-transported material.

EPOCH—A subdivision of a geologic period, such as the Pleistocene Epoch of the Quaternary Period.

ERA—A major division of geologic time. All geologic time is divided into five eras: the Archeozoic, Proterozoic, Paleozoic, Mesozoic, and Cenozoic eras.

EROSION—The process whereby loosened or dissolved materials of the earth are moved from place to place by the action of water, wind, or ice.

ERRATIC—A large boulder, deposited by glacial action, whose composition is different from that of the native bedrock.

ESCARPMENT—*See* Scarp.

EXFOLIATION—The scaling or flaking off of concentric sheets from bare rock surfaces, much like the peeling of onion layers.

EXFOLIATION DOME—A large, rounded, domal feature produced in homogeneous coarse-grained igneous rocks (and sometimes in conglomerates) by the process of exfoliation.

EXTRUSIVE—As applied to igneous rocks, rocks formed from materials ejected or poured out upon the earth's surface, such as volcanic rocks.

EXTRUSIVE ROCK—A rock that has solidified from a mass of magma that poured or was blown out upon the earth's surface.

FAULT—A fracture in a rock surface, along which there is displacement of the broken surfaces.

FAULT-BLOCK MOUNTAIN—A mountain bounded by one or more faults.

FAULTING—The movement of rock layers along a break.

FAULT SCARP—A cliff formed at the surface of a fault.

FAUNA—The forms of animal life of a particular region or time period.

FIRN—Granular ice formed by the recrystallization of snow. Intermediate between snow and glacial ice; also called *névé.*

FISSURE—An open fracture in a rock surface.

FISSURE ERUPTION—Extrusion of lava from a fissure in the earth's crust.

FJORD—A drowned glacial valley.

FLOOD PLAIN—The part of a stream valley that is covered with water during flood stage.

FLORA—The forms of plant life of a particular region or time period.

FLOWSTONE—A sedimentary rock, usually of limestone, formed by flowing water, most commonly in caverns.

FOLD—A bend in rock layers, such as an anticline or syncline.

FOLDED MOUNTAINS—Mountains that result from the folding of rocks.

FOLIATION—An extremely thin layering or laminated structure in rocks or minerals, often so pronounced as to permit separation or cleavage into thin sheets.

FORMATION—Any assemblage of rocks having some character in common, whether of origin, age, or composition. Also, anything that has been naturally formed or brought into its present shape, such as dripstones in caverns.

FOSSIL—Any remains or traces of plants or animals that have been naturally preserved in deposits of a past geologic age.

FOSSILIFEROUS—As applied to rocks, any rock containing fossils.

FOSSILIFEROUS LIMESTONE—Limestone made from the skeletons of fossilized sea animals.

FRICTION—The resistance due to surface rubbing.

FROST ACTION—Process of mechanical weathering caused by repeated cycles of freezing and thawing. Expansion of water during the freezing cycle provides the energy for the process.

FROST WEDGING—Prying off of fragments of rock by expansion of freezing water in crevices.

FUMAROLES—Fissures or holes in volcanic regions, from which steam and other volcanic gases are emitted.

GEANTICLINE—Very broad upfold in the earth's crust, extending for hundreds of miles.

GEODE—A hollow stone, usually lined or filled with mineral matter, formed by deposition in a rock cavity.

GEOLOGIC COLUMN—A chronologic arrangement of rock units in columnar form with the oldest units at the bottom and the youngest at the top.

GEOLOGIC REVOLUTIONS—Periods of marked crustal movement separating one geologic era from another.

GEOLOGIC TIME—All time that has elapsed since the first known rocks were formed, and continuing until recent, or modern, time when the glaciers of the last glaciation retreated.

GEOLOGIC TIME SCALE—A chronologic sequence of units of earth time.

GEOLOGICAL CYCLE—A period in which mountains are born and rise above the sea and are again eroded.

GEOLOGIST—A person engaged in geological work, study, or investigation.

GEOLOGY—The science that deals with the origin and nature of the earth and the development of life upon it.

GEOPHYSICS—The physics of the earth.

GEOSYNCLINE—A great, elongated downfold in which great thicknesses of sediments accumulate over a long period of time.

GEYSER—A hot spring that periodically erupts steam and hot water.

GLACIAL DRIFT—Boulders, till, gravel, sand, or clay transported by a glacier or its meltwater.

GLACIATION—A major advance of ice sheets over a large part of the earth's surface.

GLACIER—A body of ice compacted from snow, that moves under its own weight and persists from season to season.

GLACIOFLUVIAL—Pertaining to streams flowing from glaciers and their deposits.

GNEISS—A metamorphic rock, usually coarse-grained, having its mineral grains aligned in bands or foliations.

GRABEN—A trough developed when parallel faults allow the blocks between them to sink, forming broad valleys flanked on each side by steep fault scarps; also called *rift valley*.

GRADIENT—The difference in elevation between the head and mouth of a stream.

GRANITE—An intrusive igneous rock composed of orthoclase feldspar and quartz; it may contain additional minerals, most commonly mica.

GRANITIZATION—The process of alteration of other rocks into granite without actual melting.

GRANODIORITE—A coarse-grained igneous rock intermediate in composition between granite and diorite.

GRAVEL—A loose deposit of rounded, water-worn pebbles, mostly ranging in size from that of a pea to a hen's egg, and often mixed with sand.

GREENSTONE or GREENSCHIST—A metamorphosed basaltic rock having a greenish-black color.

GROUND MORAINE—Till deposited from a glacier as a veneer over the landscape and forming a gently rolling surface.

HANGING VALLEY—A tributary valley that terminates high above the floor of the main valley due to the deeper erosion of the latter; commonly by glaciation.

HEADWARD EROSION—The process whereby streams lengthen their valleys at the upper end by the cutting action of the water that flows in at the head of the valley.

HISTORICAL GEOLOGY—The branch of geology that deals with the history of the earth, including a record of life on the earth as well as physical changes in the earth itself.

HORN—A spire of bedrock left where cirques have eaten into a mountain from more than two sides around a central area. Example: Matterhorn of the Swiss Alps.

HOT SPRING—A spring that brings hot water to the surface. A thermal spring. Water temperature usually 15°F or more above mean air temperature.

ICE AGE—The glacial period, or Pleistocene Epoch of the Quaternary Period.

ICECAP—A cap of ice usually over a large area. *See also* Continental Glacier.

IGNEOUS ROCKS—Rocks formed by solidification of magma.

IMPRESSION—The form or shape left on a soft surface by objects that have come in contact with it and that may have later hardened into rock. A type of fossilization consisting of the imprint of a plant or animal structure.

INTRUSIVE IGNEOUS ROCK—Molten rock that did not reach the surface of the earth but hardened in cracks and openings in other rock layers.

INVERTEBRATES—Animals without backbones.

JASPER—Granular cryptocrystalline silica usually colored red by hematite inclusions.

JOINT—A break in a rock mass where there has been no relative movement of rock on opposite sides of the break.

JOINT SYSTEM—A series of two or more sets of joints passing through a rock mass so as to separate it into blocks of more or less regular pattern.

JURASSIC—The second, or middle, period of the Mesozoic Era.

KARST TOPOGRAPHY—A type of landscape characteristic of some limestone regions, in which drainage is mostly by means of underground streams in caverns.

KETTLE—A depression remaining after the melting of large blocks of ice buried in glacial drift.

KIPUKA—An "island" of old land left within a lava flow.

LACCOLITH—Lens-shaped body of intrusive igneous rock that has domed up the overlying rocks.

LACUSTRINE—Pertaining to a lake, sediments on a lake bottom, or sedimentary rocks composed of such material.

LANDSLIDE—The downward, rather sudden movement of a large section of land that has been loosened from a hill or mountainside.

LATERAL MORAINE—A ridge of till along the edge of a valley glacier; composed primarily of material that fell to the glacier from valley walls.

LAVA—Hot liquid rock at or close to the earth's surface, and its solidified products.

LAYER—A bed or stratum of rock.

LIMESTONE—A sedimentary rock composed largely of calcium carbonate.

LITHIFICATION—The process whereby unconsolidated rock-forming materials are converted into a consolidated or coherent state.

LOAD—The amount of material that a transporting agency, such as a stream, a glacier, or the wind, is actually carrying at a given time.

MAGMA—Molten rock deep in the earth's crust.

MANTLE ROCK—The layers of loose weathered rock lying over solid bedrock.

MARBLE—A metamorphosed, recrystallized limestone.

MARINE—Belonging to, or originating in, the sea.

MASS-WASTING—Erosional processes caused chiefly by gravity. Example: a landslide.

MEANDERS—Wide curves typical of well-developed streams.

MECHANICAL WEATHERING—The process by which rock is broken down into smaller and smaller fragments as the result of energy developed by physical forces. Also called *disintegration.*

MESA—A large, wide, flat-topped hill, usually a remnant of horizontal beds.

MESOZOIC—The geologic era between the Paleozoic and Cenozoic eras; the "Age of Reptiles"; contains the Triassic, Jurassic, and Cretaceous periods.

METAMORPHIC ROCKS—Rocks that have been changed from their original form by great heat and pressure.

METAMORPHISM—The process whereby rocks are changed by heat, pressure, or chemical environment into different kinds.

MINERAL—A natural, inorganic substance having distinct physical properties, and a composition expressed by a chemical formula.

MINERALOGIST—A geologist who specializes in studying minerals.

MINERALOGY—The subdivision of geology that deals with the study of minerals.

MIOCENE—Fourth-oldest epoch of the Tertiary Period of the Cenozoic Era.

MISSISSIPPIAN—The fifth period of the Paleozoic Era.

MONADNOCK—A residual hill or higher elevation left standing on a peneplain after erosion of the surrounding material.

MORAINE—A ridge or mound of boulders, gravel, sand, and clay carried on or deposited by a glacier.

MOUNTAIN GLACIER—Synonymous with alpine glacier.

MUD CRACKS—Cracks caused by the shrinkage of a drying deposit of silt or clay under surface conditions.

NATIONAL MONUMENT—An area set aside by the President of the United States or by act of Congress because of its scientific or historical value, and administered by the National Park Service.

NATIONAL PARK—An area of greater importance, and usually of greater extent, than a national monument, set aside by act of Congress, most commonly because of its scenic and geologic interest.

NÉVÉ—Compacted granular snow partly converted into ice; also called *firn*.

NUÉE ARDENTE—Avalanche of fiery ash enveloped in compressed gas from a volcanic eruption.

OBSIDIAN—A glassy rock formed from hardened lava, found just under the foamy top layer.

OLIGOCENE—Third-oldest epoch of the Tertiary Period of the Cenozoic Era.

ONYX—A translucent variety of quartz consisting of differently colored bands, often used as a decorative stone. Also, applied to similarly appearing varieties of calcite or limestone, such as dripstones and flowstones of caverns, and used for similar purposes.

OPAL—Amorphous silica, with varying amounts of water. A mineral gel.

ORDOVICIAN—The second period of the Paleozoic Era.

ORGANISM—Anything possessing life; a plant or animal body.

OROGENY—A major disturbance or mountain-building movement in the earth's crust.

OUTCROP—An exposure of bedrock at the surface of the ground.

OUTWASH—Stratified sediments laid down by the meltwater of a glacier beyond the glacier itself.

OUTWASH PLAINS—Plains formed by the deposition of materials washed out from the edges of a glacier.

OVERHANG—The upper portion of a cliff extending beyond the lower.

OXIDATION—The chemical combination of substances with oxygen.

PAHOEHOE LAVA—Lava that has solidified with a smooth, ropy, or billowy appearance.

PALEOBOTANY—The branch of paleontology that deals with the study of fossil plants.

PALEOCENE—Oldest epoch of the Tertiary Period of the Cenozoic Era.

PALEOGEOGRAPHY—The study of ancient geography.

PALEONTOLOGY—The branch of geology that deals with the study of fossil plants and animals.

PALEONTOLOGIST—A scientist who studies fossils.

PALEOZOIC—The era of geologic time that contains the Cambrian, Ordovician, Silurian, Devonian, Mississippian, Pennsylvanian, and Permian periods.

PARASITIC CONES—Volcanic cones developed at openings some distance below the main vent.

PASS—A deep gap or passageway through a mountain range.

PEAK—The topmost point, or summit, of a mountain.

PEBBLE—A smooth, rounded stone, larger than sand and smaller than a hen's egg.

PEDIMENT—Broad, smooth erosional surface developed at the expense of a highland mass in an arid climate; underlain by beveled rock, which is covered by a veneer of gravel and rock debris.

PELE'S HAIR—Volcanic glass spun out into hairlike form.

PENEPLAIN—Extensive land surface eroded to a nearly flat plain.

PENEPLANATION—The process of erosion to base level over a vast area, which results in the production of a peneplain.

PENNSYLVANIAN—The sixth period of the Paleozoic Era.

PERIOD—A main division of a geologic era characterized primarily by its distinctive remains of life.

PERMAFROST—Permanently frozen subsoil.

PERMEABILITY—The degree to which water can penetrate and pass through rock.

PERMIAN—The seventh and last period of the Paleozoic Era.

PETRIFACTION—A process in which the original substance of a fossil is replaced by mineral matter.

PETROLOGY—The scientific study of rocks.

PIEDMONT—The area of land at the base of a mountain. That portion of the Appalachian Region that lies alongside the eastern side of the Blue Ridge.

PIEDMONT GLACIER—A glacier formed by the coalescence of alpine glaciers and spreading over plains at the feet of the mountains from which the alpine glaciers came.

PILLAR—A column of rock in a cavern produced by the union of a stalactite and a stalagmite. Also, any column of rock remaining after erosion of the surrounding rock.

PILLOW LAVA—A basaltic lava that develops a structure resembling a pile of pillows when it solidifies under water.

PIPE (volcanic)—The tube leading to a volcano, sometimes filled with solidified material.

PIT CRATER—A crater formed by sinking in of the surface; not primarily a vent for lava.

PLAIN—A region of horizontal rock layers that has low relief due to a comparatively low elevation.

PLASTIC DEFORMATION—The folding or flowing of solid rock under conditions of great heat and pressure.

PLATEAU—A region of horizontal rock layers that has high relief due to higher elevation.

PLATEAU BASALT—Basalt poured out from fissures in floods that tend to form great plateaus; also called flood basalt.

PLEISTOCENE—The first of the two epochs of the Quaternary Period, and that which precedes modern time, known also as the Great Ice Age.

PLIOCENE—Last epoch of the Tertiary Period of the Cenozoic Era.

PLUTONIC—Applied to rocks that have formed at great depths below the surface.

PLUTONIC ROCKS—*See* Intrusive Igneous Rock.

PORPHYRY—A mineral texture of fairly large crystals set in a mass of very fine crystals.

POTHOLE—A rounded depression in the rock of a stream bed.

PRECAMBRIAN—A collective name covering the Archeozoic and Proterozoic eras and the rocks formed during those eras.

PRECIPITATED ROCKS—Sedimentary rocks formed by the precipitation of mineral matter out of solution, such as limestone or dolomite.

PROTEROZOIC—The second of the geologic eras, also called Late Precambrian.

PUMICE—A froth of volcanic glass.

PRYOCLASTIC ROCK—Fragmental rock blown out by volcanic explosion and deposited from the air; for example, bomb, cinder, ash, tuff, and pumice.

QUARTZ—One of the main rock-forming minerals, composed of pure silica.

QUARTZITE—A hard metamorphic rock composed essentially of quartz sand cemented by silica.

QUATERNARY—The second and last period of the Cenozoic Era. It includes the Pleistocene Epoch, or Ice Age, and all the time since.

RAPIDS—Stretches in a stream where the water drops over rock ledges or accumulations of loose rock, churning itself into foam and making navigation dangerous or impossible.

RECENT—All time since the close of the Pleistocene Epoch, or Ice Age.

REGIONAL METAMORPHISM—The alteration of rocks over a very large area due to some major geological process.

REJUVENATION—Any action that tends to increase the gradient of a stream.

RELIEF—The difference in elevation between the high and low places of a land surface.

REPLACEMENT—The formation of mineral replicas of organic remains by the exchange of minerals for cell contents.

RESIDUAL BOULDERS—Large rock fragments formed in place by weathering of the solid bedrock.

REVOLUTION—A time of major mountain building, bringing an end to a geologic period or era.

RIFT—A large fracture in the earth's crust.

RIFT VALLEY—A major topographical feature produced by the dropping down of a long segment of the earth's crust between two parallel faults.

RIFT ZONES—The highly fractured belts on flanks of volcanoes along which most of the eruptions take place.

RIPPLE MARKS—Wavelike corrugations produced in unconsolidated materials by wind or water.

ROCHES MOUTONNÉES—Bedrock that has been smoothed and "plucked" by the passage of glacial ice.

ROCK—Any natural mass of mineral matter, usually consisting of a mixture of two or more minerals; it constitutes an essential part of the earth's crust.

ROCK FLOUR—Finely ground rock particles, chiefly silt size, resulting from glacial abrasion.

ROCK GLACIER—An accumulation of rocky material moving slowly down a valley in the manner of a glacier.

ROCK WASTE—Fragments of bedrock produced by weathering.

RUNOFF—The water that flows on the ground surface, tending to drain through streams toward the sea.

SANDSTONE—Sedimentary rock composed of largely cemented sand grains, usually quartz.

SCARP—A steep rise in the ground produced either by the outcrop of a resistant rock or by the line of a fault.

SCHIST—A finely layered metamorphic rock that splits easily.

SCORIA—Slaglike fragment of lava explosively ejected from a volcanic vent.

SEA CAVE—Cave formed as a result of erosion by sea waves.

SEA CLIFF—Cliff formed by marine erosion.

SEDIMENT—Solid material suspended in water, wind, or ice; such material transported from its place of origin and redeposited elsewhere.

SEDIMENTARY ROCKS—Rocks formed by the accumulation of sediment derived from the breakdown of earlier rocks, by chemical precipitation, or by organic activity.

SEISMOGRAPH—An instrument that detects and records earthquake waves.

SEISMOLOGIST—A person who studies and interprets the effects of earthquake activity.

SHALE—A sedimentary rock formed by the hardening of mud and clay, and usually tending to split into thin sheets or layers.

SHEET WASH—A type of erosion in which water strips away exposed topsoil slowly and evenly on a slope.

SHIELD VOLCANO—A volcano having the shape of a very broad, gently sloping dome.

SILICA—The chemical compound of oxygen and silicon, which are the two commonest elements in the earth's crust.

SILL—A sheet of intrusive rock lying parallel to the bedding of the rock that is intruded.

SILT—Soil particles intermediate in size between clay particles and sand grains.

SILURIAN—The third period of the Paleozoic Era.

SINK—A depression in the earth's surface formed by the collapse of the roof of an underground cavern.

SLATE—A metamorphosed clay rock with a pronounced cleavage along which it readily splits.

SLIDE-ROCK—*See* Talus.

SOIL—Layers of decomposed rock and organic materials on the surface of the land areas of the earth.

SOLFATARA—A fumarole liberating sulfur-bearing gas.

SPATTER CONES—Small cones that form in lava fields away from the main vent. Lava is spattered out of them through holes in a thin crust.

SPELEOLOGY—The scientific study of caverns and related features.

SPELEOTHEM—A secondary mineral deposit formed in caves; for example, a stalagmite or a stalactite.

SPRING—Water issuing from beneath the surface through a natural opening in sufficient quantity to make a distinct current.

STACK—An isolated column of rock left standing as waves erode a shoreline.

STALACTITE—A stony projection from the roof of a cavern, formed of minerals deposited from dripping water.

STALAGMITE—A raised deposit on the floor of a cavern, formed by minerals deposited from dripping water.

STRATA—Rock layers or beds.

STRATIFICATION—The structure produced by the deposition of sediments in beds or layers.

STRATIFIED ROCKS—Rocks which occur in parallel layers.

STRATIGRAPHY—The study of rock layers.

STRATUM (pl. Strata)—A rock layer or bed.

STRATOVOLCANO—A volcano having a cone of alternate layers of lava and solid fragments.

STRIAE—Scratches on the surface of rocks resulting from the movement of glacial ice.

STRUCTURAL GEOLOGY—The study of rocks and their relationships.

SUBMERGENCE—The flooding of land by the sea. Characteristic of most geologic periods.

SUBSIDENCE—Sinking of the earth's crust.

SYNCLINE—A fold of layers of rock that dip inward from both sides toward the axis; opposite of anticline.

SYNCLINORIUM—A broad regional syncline on which are superimposed minor folds.

SYSTEM—The rocks that accumulated during a period of geologic time.

TAIGA—A type of vegetation characteristic of subarctic climates.

TALUS—A mass of rock debris at the base of a steep mountain or cliff; also called *scree*.

TECTONICS—The phenomena associated with rock deformation and rock structures generally; the study of these phenomena.

TEMBLOR—An earthquake.

TERTIARY—The first of the two periods of the Cenozoic Era; commonly called the "Age of Mammals."

TEXTURE—The composite arrangement, shape, and size of the grains or crystal particles of a rock.

TILL—Glacial deposits that have not been stratified or sorted by water action.

TILLITE—A sedimentary rock composed of firmly consolidated till.

TOPOGRAPHIC MAP—A map showing surface features of a portion of the earth.

TOPOGRAPHY—The relief and contour of the land surface.

TRANSPORT—The carrying by water, wind, or ice from one place to another.

TRAP—Old name for a lava flow.

TRAVERTINE—A variety of limestone deposited by dripping or flowing water in caverns or by springs, as in stalactites and stalagmites.

TRIASSIC—Oldest period of the Mesozoic Era.

TRIBUTARY—A stream that flows into a larger one.

TRILOBITES—An extinct group of arthropods, possibly related to the crustaceans, with a trilobed dorsal skeleton.

TROUGH—A channel or long depression between two ridges of land.

TUNDRA—A type of climate in the zone of transition between the subarctic regions and the icecaps.

UNCONFORMITY—A break in the sequence of rock formations that separates younger groups from older ones; caused primarily by removal of some of the older rocks by erosion before those of a later sequence were laid down.

UNIFORMITARIANISM—The doctrine that the past geological record can be interpreted by reference to present-day phenomena and processes. "The present is the key to the past."

UPLIFT—The elevation of any extensive part of the earth's surface from a lower position by some geologic force.

VALLEY—A long depression on the earth's surface, usually bounded by hills or mountains, and typically traversed by a stream that receives the drainage from the adjacent heights.

VALLEY TRAIN—The deposit of rock material carried down by a stream originating from a glacier confined in a narrow valley.

VEIN—A thin and usually irregular igneous intrusion.

VENT—An opening where volcanic material reaches the surface.

VENTIFACT—A stone that has been smoothed by wind abrasion.

VERTEBRATES—Animals with backbones.

VESICULAR—Having bubble holes formed by gases.

VOLCANIC—Pertaining to volcanoes or any rocks associated with volcanic activity at or below the surface.

VOLCANIC NECK—A rock plug formed in the passageway of a volcano when magma slowly cools and solidifies there.

VOLCANISM—A general term including all types of activity due to movement of magma.

VOLCANO—The vent from which molten rock materials reach the surface, together with the accumulations of volcanic materials deposited around the vent.

WARPING—The bending of sedimentary beds of rock into broad, low domes and shallow basins.

WATERFALL—The dropping of a stream of water over a vertical or nearly vertical descent in its course.

WATER GAP—A valley that cuts across a mountain ridge, through which the stream still flows.

WATER TABLE—The upper boundary of the ground-water, below which all spaces within the rock are completely filled with water.

WAVE-BUILT TERRACE—A seaward extension of a wave-cut terrace, produced by debris from wave action.

WAVE-CUT TERRACE—A level surface of rock under the water along the shore, formed as waves cut back the shoreline.

WEATHERING—The natural disintegration and decomposition of rocks and minerals.

YOSEMITE—A glacially carved, U-shaped, steep-walled canyon.

Selected Bibliography

Many readers will want to learn more about geology in general, or about the geology of some particular national park. The following list includes selected references of many types, any one of which contains additional information on various phases of geology and the national parks. This list is by no means all-inclusive, and many other interesting and worth-while publications may be found in public, school, and college libraries. The publications are grouped together according to subject matter, each list consisting of author, date of publication, title, and publisher.

Those readers who want a more comprehensive list of earth-science references will find it helpful to consult the following publications:

MATTHEWS, WILLIAM H., III, 1964. *Selected References for Earth Science Courses* (ESCP Reference Series Pamphlet RS-2). Prentice-Hall, Inc., Englewood Cliffs, New Jersey 07632

MATTHEWS, WILLIAM H., III, 1965. *Selected Maps and Earth Science Publications for the States and Provinces of North America* (ESCP Reference Series Pamphlet RS-4). Prentice-Hall, Inc., Englewood Cliffs, New Jersey 07632

PANGBORN, MARK W., JR., 1957. *Earth for the Layman: A List of Nearly 1400 Good Books and Pamphlets of Popular Interest on Geology, Mining, Oil, Maps, and Related Subjects.* American Geological Institute, 1444 N Street, N.W., Washington, D.C. 20005

Specific Parks

In addition to the selected publications listed below, the National Park Service issues descriptive brochures and other informational material about each of the parks. These may be obtained by writing the superintendents of the respective parks at the addresses listed in Appendix B.

BRYCE CANYON NATIONAL PARK

GRATER, R. K., 1950. *Guide to Zion, Bryce Canyon, and Cedar Breaks.* Binfords & Mort, 2505 S.E. 11 Ave., Portland, Oregon 97242

GREGORY, HERBERT E., 1951. *The Geology and Geography of the Paunsaugunt Region, Utah.* Geological Survey Professional Paper 226, U.S. Government Printing Office, Washington, D.C. 20402

CANYONLANDS NATIONAL PARK

KING, P. E., 1948. *Geology of the Southern Guadalupe Mountains, Texas.* Geological Survey Professional Paper 215, U.S. Government Printing Office, Washington, D.C. 20402

NEWELL, N. D., and others, 1953. *The Permian Reef Complex of the Guadalupe Mountains Region, Texas and New Mexico.* W. H. Freeman & Co., San Francisco, California 94104

ROSE, R. H., 1965. "Upheaval Dome." *National Parks Magazine* (Vol. 39, No. 216, pp. 11–16), 1300 New Hampshire Ave., N.W., Washington, D.C. 20036

ROSWELL GEOLOGICAL SOCIETY, 1964. *Geology of the Capitan Reef Complex of the Guadalupe Mountains.* Roswell Geological Society, Box 1171, Roswell, New Mexico 88201

SPANGLE, PAUL (editor), 1960. *Guidebook to Carlsbad Caverns National Park.* Carlsbad Caverns Natural History Association, Box 1598, Carlsbad, New Mexico 88220

Western Gateways magazine, 1964. "Canyonlands Highway Issue." KC Publications, Box 428, Flagstaff, Arizona 86001

CRATER LAKE NATIONAL PARK

BALDWIN, EWART M., 1964. *Geology of Oregon.* J. W. Edwards, Ann Arbor, Michigan 48103

CONTOR, ROGER J., 1963. *The Underworld of Oregon Caves.* Crater Lake Natural History Association, Inc., Crater Lake, Oregon 97604

MACKIN, J. HOOVER, and CARY, S. A., 1965. *Origin of Cascade Landscapes.* Information Circular No. 41, Washington Division of Mines and Geology, Olympia, Washington 98501

RUHLE, GEORGE C., 1964. *Along Crater Lake Roads.* Crater Lake Natural History Association, Inc., Crater Lake, Oregon 97604

WILLIAMS, HOWEL, 1942. *The Geology of Crater Lake National Park, Oregon.* Publication No. 540, Carnegie Institution of Washington, Washington, D.C. 20005

WILLIAMS, HOWEL, 1948. *The Ancient Volcanoes of Oregon.* University of Oregon Press, Eugene, Oregon 97403

WILLIAMS, HOWEL, 1957. *Crater Lake, the Story of its Origin.* University of California Press, Berkeley, California 94720

GLACIER NATIONAL PARK

BEATTY, M. E., 1958. *Motorist's Guide to the Going-to-the-Sun Road.* Glacier Natural History Association, West Glacier, Montana 59936

DYSON, J. L., 1960. *The Geologic Story of Glacier National Park.* Glacier Natural History Association, West Glacier, Montana 59936

DYSON, J. L., 1962. *Glaciers and Glaciation in Glacier National Park.* Glacier Natural History Association, West Glacier, Montana 59936

ROSS, C. P., 1959. *Geology of Glacier National Park and the Flathead Region Northwestern Montana.* Geological Survey Professional Paper 296, U.S. Government Printing Office, Washington, D.C. 20402

ROSS, C. P., and REZAK, RICHARD, 1959. *The Rocks and Fossils of Glacier National Park: The Story of Their Origin.* Geological Survey Paper 294-K, U.S. Government Printing Office, Washington, D.C. 20402

RUHLE, G. C., 1963. *Guide to Glacier National Park.* John W. Forney, Northstar Center, Minneapolis, Minnesota

GRAND CANYON NATIONAL PARK

DARTON, N. H., 1961. *Story of the Grand Canyon of Arizona —How It Was Made* (33rd ed.). Fred Harvey, Grand Canyon, Arizona 86023

DUTTON, C. E., 1882. *Tertiary History of the Grand Cañon District.* Government Printing Office, Washington, D.C. 20402

KRUTCH, J. W., 1962. *Grand Canyon.* The Natural History Library, Doubleday & Co., Garden City, New York 11530

MAXSON, J. H., 1961. *Grand Canyon—Origin and Scenery.* Bulletin 13, Grand Canyon Natural History Association, Box 219, Grand Canyon, Arizona 86023

MCKEE, E. D., 1965. *Ancient Landscapes of the Grand Canyon Region* (23d ed.). Grand Canyon Natural History Association, Box 219, Grand Canyon, Arizona 86023

POWELL, J. W., 1895. *Canyons of the Colorado.* Republished in 1961 by Dover Publications, New York, New York 10014, under the title *The Exploration of the Colorado River and Its Canyons.*

SUTTON, A. and M., 1971. *The Wilderness World of the Grand Canyon.* J. B. Lippincott Co., Philadelphia, Pennsylvania 19105

GRAND TETON NATIONAL PARK

BONNEY, O. H., and BONNEY, L. G., 1961. *Bonney's Guide: Jackson's Hole and Grand Teton National Park.* Orrin H. Bonney and Lorraine G. Bonney, 1309 American Investors Bldg., Houston, Texas 77002

FRYXELL, F. M., 1959. *The Tetons—Interpretations of a Mountain Landscape.* Grand Teton Natural History Association, Moose, Wyoming 83012

LOVE, J. D., and REED, JOHN C., JR., 1967. *Creation of the Teton Landscape.* Grand Teton Natural History Association, Moose, Wyoming 83012

HALEAKALA NATIONAL PARK

See Hawaii Volcanoes National Park

HAWAII VOLCANOES NATIONAL PARK

MACDONALD, G. A., and HUBBARD, D. H., 1965. *Volcanoes of the National Parks in Hawaii.* Hawaii Natural History Association, Hawaii Volcanoes National Park, Hawaii 96718

STEARNS, H. T., 1966. *Geology of the State of Hawaii.* Pacific Books, Box 558, Palo Alto, California 94302

KINGS CANYON NATIONAL PARK

See Sequoia-Kings Canyon National Parks

LASSEN VOLCANIC NATIONAL PARK

LOOMIS, B. F., 1966. *Eruptions of Lassen Peak* (3d ed.). Loomis Museum Association, Lassen Volcanic National Park, Mineral, California 96063

SCHULZ, P. E., 1959. *Geology of Lassen's Landscape.* Loomis Museum Association, Lassen Volcanic National Park, Mineral, California 96063

MESA VERDE NATIONAL PARK

BURNS, W. A., 1960. *The Natural History of the Southwest.* Franklin Watts, New York, New York 10022

WANEK, A. A., 1959. *Geology and Fuel Resources of the Mesa Verde Area, Montezuma and La Plata Counties, Colorado.* Geological Survey Bulletin 1072-M, U.S. Government Printing Office, Washington, D.C. 20402

WATSON, DON (no date). *Cliff Dwellings of the Mesa Verde.* Mesa Verde Museum Association, Box 38, Mesa Verde National Park, Colorado 81330

MOUNT McKINLEY NATIONAL PARK

BROOKS, A. H., 1911. *The Mount McKinley Region, Alaska.* Geological Survey Professional Paper 70, U.S. Government Printing Office, Washington, D.C. 20402

MURIE, ADOLPH, 1961. *A Naturalist in Alaska.* The Devin-Adair Co., Old Greenwich, Connecticut 06870

REED, J. C., 1961. *Geology of the Mount McKinley Quadrangle, Alaska.* Geological Survey Bulletin 1108-A, U.S. Government Printing Office, Washington, D.C. 20402

MOUNT RAINIER NATIONAL PARK

COOMBS, H. A., 1936. "The Geology of Mount Rainier National Park." Washington University Publications in Geology (Vol. 3, No. 2) Seattle, Washington 98105

CRANDELL, D. R., and FAHNESTOCK, R. K., 1965. *Rockfalls and Avalanches from Little Tahoma Peak on Mount Rainier, Washington.* Geological Survey Bulletin 1221-A, U.S. Government Printing Office, Washington, D.C. 20402

FISKE, R. S., HOPSON, C. A., and WATERS, A. C., 1963. *Geology of Mount Rainier National Park, Washington.* Geological Survey Professional Paper 444, U.S. Government Printing Office, Washington, D.C. 20402

GRATER, R. K., 1949. *Grater's Guide to Mount Rainier National Park.* Binfords & Mort, 2505 S.E. 11 Ave., Portland, Oregon 97242

STAGNER, HOWARD, 1952. *Behind the Scenery of Mount Rainier National Park.* Mount Rainier Natural History Association, Longmire, Washington 98397

OLYMPIC NATIONAL PARK

DANNER, W. R., 1955. *Geology of Olympic National Park.* University of Washington Press, Seattle, Washington 98105, and Olympic Natural History Association, Port Angeles, Washington 98362

FAGERLUND, G. O., 1954. *Olympic National Park.* Natural History Handbook No. 1, U.S. Government Printing Office, Washington, D.C. 20402

KIRK, RUTH, 1964. *Exploring the Olympic Peninsula.* University of Washington Press, Seattle, Washington 98105, and Olympic Natural History Association, Port Angeles, Washington 98362

PETRIFIED FOREST NATIONAL PARK

Arizona Highways Magazine, 1963. "Petrified Forest National Parks Issue," Arizona Highway Department, Phoenix, Arizona 85009

BRODERICK, HAROLD, 1951. *Agatized Rainbows: A Story of the Petrified Forest.* Petrified Forest Museum Association, Holbrook, Arizona 86025

ROCKY MOUNTAIN NATIONAL PARK

ALBERTS, E. C., 1954. *Rocky Mountain National Park, Colorado.* Natural History Handbook No. 3, U.S. Government Printing Office, Washington, D.C. 20402

ROCKY MOUNTAIN NATURE ASSOCIATION, 1959. *Glaciers in Rocky Mountain National Park.* Rocky Mountain Nature Association, Estes Park, Colorado 80517

WEGEMANN, C. H., 1961. *A Guide to the Geology of Rocky Mountain National Park.* U.S. Government Printing Office, Washington, D.C. 20402

ZIM, H. S., 1964. *The Rocky Mountains.* Golden Press, New York, New York 10022

SEQUOIA-KINGS CANYON NATIONAL PARKS

COOK, L. F., 1955. *The Giant Sequoias of California* (rev. ed.). U.S. Government Printing Office, Washington, D.C. 20402

FRYXELL, F. M., 1962. *François Matthes and the Marks of Time.* Sierra Club, 1050 Mills Tower, San Francisco, California 94100

MATTHES, F. E., 1956. *Sequoia National Park—A Geological Album.* University of California Press, Berkeley, California 94700

MATTHES, F. E., 1965. *Glacial Reconnaissance of Sequoia National Park.* Geological Survey Professional Paper 504-A, U.S. Government Printing Office, Washington, D.C. 20402

OBERHANSLEY, F. R., 1965. *Crystal Cave in Sequoia National Park* (rev. ed.). Sequoia Natural History Association, Three Rivers, California 93271

STORER, TRACY, and USINGER, ROBERT, 1963. *Sierra Nevada Natural History.* University of California Press, Berkeley, California 94700

WHITE, J. R., and PUSATERI, SAMUEL, 1965. *Illustrated Guide—Sequoia and Kings Canyon National Parks* (rev. ed.). Stanford University Press, Stanford, California 94305

YELLOWSTONE NATIONAL PARK

BAUER, C. M., 1962. *Yellowstone—Its Underworld. Geology and Historical Anecdotes of Our Oldest National Park.* University of New Mexico Press, Albuquerque, New Mexico 87106

CHITTENDEN, HIRAM, 1933. *Yellowstone National Park.* Stanford University Press, Stanford, California 94305. (Republished in 1964 by the University of Oklahoma Press, Norman, Oklahoma 73069.)

DOUGLASS, I. B., 1939. *Some Chemical Features of Yellowstone National Park.* (Reprinted from *Journal of Chemical Education,* Vol. 16, No. 9). Yellowstone Library and Museum Association, Yellowstone National Park, Wyoming 83020

FISCHER, W. A., 1960. *Yellowstone's Living Geology.* Yellowstone Library and Museum Association, Yellowstone National Park, Wyoming 83020

HAYNES, J. E., 1961. *Haynes' Guide: A Handbook of Yellowstone National Park.* Haynes Studios, Bozeman, Montana 59715

LINK, L. W., 1964. *Great Montana Earthquake.* L. W. Link, Cardwell, Montana 59721

MARLER, G. D., 1963. *The Story of Old Faithful Geyser.* Yellowstone Library and Museum Association, Yellowstone National Park, Wyoming 83020

MARLER, G. D., 1964. *Studies of Geysers and Hot Springs Along the Firehole River.* Yellowstone Library and Museum Association, Yellowstone National Park, Wyoming 83020

WITKIND, I. J., 1962. *The Night the Earth Shook.* U.S. Department of Agriculture, Forest Service, Misc. Publication No. 907, U.S. Government Printing Office, Washington, D.C. 20402

YOSEMITE NATIONAL PARK

BEATTY, M. E., 1943. *Brief Story of the Geology of Yosemite Valley.* Yosemite Natural History Association, Box 545, Yosemite National Park, California 95389

BROCKMAN, C. F., 1945. *Falls of Yosemite and Famous Waterfalls of the World.* Yosemite Natural History Association, Box 545, Yosemite National Park, California 95389

GOLDSTEIN, MILTON, 1972. *The Magnificent West: Yosemite.* Doubleday & Company, Inc., Garden City, New York 11530

HUNTINGTON, H. E., 1966. *The Yosemite Story.* Doubleday & Co., Garden City, New York 11530

MATTHES, F. E., 1930. *Geologic History of the Yosemite Valley.* Geological Survey Professional Paper 160, U.S. Government Printing Office, Washington, D.C. 20402

MATTHES, F. E., 1950. *The Incomparable Valley.* University of California Press, Berkeley, California 94700

MUIR, JOHN, 1962. *The Yosemite.* The Natural History Library, Doubleday & Co., Garden City, New York 11530

ZION NATIONAL PARK

BRUHN, A. F., 1962. *Southern Utah's Land of Color.* Zion Natural History Association, Springdale, Utah 84767

GRATER, R. K., 1950. *Guide to Zion, Bryce Canyon, and Cedar Breaks.* Binfords & Mort, 2505 S.E. 11 Ave., Portland, Oregon 97242

GREGORY, H. E., 1940. *Geologic and Geographic Sketches of Zion and Bryce Canyon National Parks.* Zion Natural History Association, Springdale, Utah 84767

GREGORY, H. E., 1950. *Geology and Geography of the Zion Park Region, Utah and Arizona.* Geological Survey Professional Paper 220, U.S. Government Printing Office, Washington, D.C. 20402

General

ALBRIGHT, H. M., and TAYLOR, F. J., 1946. *Oh, Ranger!* Dodd, Mead & Co., New York, New York 10016

BOLIN, L. A., 1962. *The National Parks of the United States.* Alfred A. Knopf, New York, New York 10022

BUTCHER, DEVEREUX, 1956. *Exploring Our National Parks and Monuments* (5th ed.). Houghton Mifflin Company, Boston, Massachusetts 02107

BUTCHER, DEVEREUX, 1965. *Our National Parks in Color.* Clarkson N. Potter, New York, New York 10016

FALK, GENE, and O'HARA, MICHAEL, 1965. *National Parks Summer Jobs.* O'Hara/Falk-Research, Box 4495, Fresno, California

HEATH, MONROE, 1959. *Our National Parks at a Glance.* Pacific Coast Publishers, Campbell Ave. at Scott Dr., Menlo Park, California 94026

ISE, JOHN, 1961. *Our National Park Policy: A Critical History.* Johns Hopkins Press, Baltimore, Maryland 21218

JENSEN, PAUL, 1964. *National Parks: A Guide to the National Parks and Monuments of the United States.* Golden Press, New York, New York 10022

LOBSENZ, NORMAN, 1959. *The First Book of National Parks.* Franklin Watts, New York, New York 10022

MELBO, I. R., 1960. *Our Country's National Parks* (2 vols.). The Bobbs-Merrill Company, Indianapolis, Indiana 46206

EDITORS, NATIONAL GEOGRAPHIC SOCIETY, 1959. *America's Wonderlands—The Scenic National Parks and Monuments of the United States.* The National Geographic Society, Washington, D.C. 20036

NATIONAL PARK SERVICE, 1964. *Parks for America: A Survey of Park and Related Resources in the Fifty States, and a Preliminary Plan.* U.S. Government Printing Office, Washington, D.C. 20402

SHANKLAND, ROBERT, 1951. *Steve Mather of the National Parks.* Alfred A. Knopf, New York, New York 10022

STORY, ISABELLE F., 1957. *The National Park Story in Pictures.* U.S. Government Printing Office, Washington, D.C. 20402

EDITORS, SUNSET BOOKS AND SUNSET MAGAZINE, 1965. *National Parks of the West.* Lane Magazine and Book Co., Menlo Park, California 94025

SUTTON, ANN, and SUTTON, MYRON, 1965. *Guarding the Treasured Lands: The Story of the National Park Service.* J. B. Lippincott Company, Philadelphia, Pennsylvania 19105

THOMSON, PETER, 1961. *Wonders of Our National Parks.* Dodd, Mead & Co., New York, New York 10016

TILDEN, FREEMAN, 1961. *The National Parks: What They Mean to You and Me.* Alfred A. Knopf, New York, New York 10022

UDALL, STEWART L., 1963. *The Quiet Crisis.* Holt, Rinehart & Winston, New York, New York 10017

UDALL, STEWART L., 1966. *The National Parks of America.* Country Beautiful Foundation, 24198 Bluemound Rd., Waukesha, Wisconsin 53186.

YEAGER, DORR, 1959. *National Parks in California.* Lane Magazine and Book Co., Menlo Park, California 94025

Nontechnical Geological References

AMERICAN GEOLOGICAL INSTITUTE, 1962. *A Dictionary of Geological Terms.* Dolphin Books, Doubleday & Co., Garden City, New York 11530

CHAMBERLAIN, BARBARA B., 1964. *These Fragile Outposts—A Geological Look at Cape Cod, Martha's Vineyard, and Nantucket.* The Natural History Press, Garden City, New York 11530

FARB, PETER, 1962. *Face of North America.* Harper & Row, New York, New York 10016

LEET, L. D., and LEET, F. J., 1961. *The World of Geology.* McGraw-Hill Book Co., New York, New York 10036

MATHER, K. F., 1964. *The Earth Beneath Us.* Random House, New York, New York 10022

MATTHEWS, WILLIAM H., III, 1962. *Fossils: An Introduction to Prehistoric Life.* Barnes & Noble, New York, New York 10003

MATTHEWS, WILLIAM H., III, 1967. *Geology Made Simple.* Made Simple Books, Doublday & Co., Garden City, New York 11530

PEARL, RICHARD M., 1960. *Geology.* Barnes & Noble, New York, New York 10003

SHELTON, JOHN S., 1966. *Geology Illustrated.* W. H. Freeman & Co., San Francisco, California 94104

SHIMER, J. A., 1959. *This Sculptured Earth: The Landscape of America.* Columbia University Press, New York, New York 10027

STRAHLER, A. N., 1966. *A Geologist's View of Cape Cod.* The Natural History Press, Garden City, New York 11530

WYCKOFF, JEROME, 1960. *The Story of Geology.* Golden Press, New York, New York 10022

Theodore Roosevelt's Tribute to the Canyon

On May 6, 1903, President Theodore Roosevelt paid tribute to the Canyon in a speech delivered at the Canyon. In 1908 he acted upon his sentiments by declaring the Canyon a National Monument. The Grand Canyon National Park was created by an Act of Congress in 1919. We have not completely followed the President's advice, but, fortunately, we are determined, basically, to "leave it as it is" so that our "children's children will get the benefit of it."

In the Grand Canyon, Arizona has a natural wonder which, so far as I know, is in kind absolutely unparalleled throughout the rest of the world. I want to ask you to do one thing in connection with it in your own interest and in the interest of the country—to keep this great wonder of nature as it now is. I was delighted to learn of the wisdom of the Santa Fe railroad people in deciding not to build their hotel on the brink of the Canyon. I hope you will not have a building of any kind, not a summer cottage, a hotel or anything else, to mar the wonderful grandeur, the sublimity, the great loveliness and beauty of the Canyon. Leave it as it is. You cannot improve on it. The ages have been at work on it, and man can only mar it. What you can do is to keep it for your children, your children's children, and for all who come after you, as one of the great rights which every American if he can travel at all should see. We have gotten past the stage, my fellow citizens, when we are to be pardoned if we treat any part of our country as something to be skinned for two or three years for the use of the present generation, whether it be the forest, the water, the scenery. Whatever it is, handle it so that your children's children will get the benefit of it.

Index

A NOTE ON DYE TRANSFER PRINTS

Information about signed original dye transfer prints of any of the
pictures in the book may be obtained by writing to:

Milton Goldstein
P.O. Box 3745, Olympic Station
Beverly Hills, California 90212

GRAND CANYON
NATIONAL
MONUMENT

Kanab Creek

Tapeats Creek

GREAT THUMB
MESA

*Chikapanagi
Point*

Colorado River

POWELL PLATEAU

*Towago
Point*

Havasu Creek

GRANITE GORGE

Shinumo

HAVASUPAI
INDIAN
RESERVATION

Apache Point

*Havasupai
Point*

TRAIL

*Hualapai
Hilltop*

Hopi Point   Powell Memorial

*Mohave
Point*

Yavapai Point

COCON...

*Mather
Point*

*Yavapai
Museum*

BRIGHT ANGEL TRAIL

TRAIL

EAST RIM DRIVE

WEST RIM DRIVE

*Park Headquarters
Visitor Center*

TRAIL

*Railroad
Station*

*Shrine of
the Ages*

*Yavapai
Lodge*

GRAND CANYON
VILLAGE
Visitor Center

Parking

*Post
Office*

*Trailer
Village*

*Motor
Lodge*

Service

Maintenance

Campground

Hospital

0   ½   1 MILE

Morris

Grand Canyon
National Park

MARBLE CANYON
NATIONAL
MONUMENT

NAVAJO
INDIAN
RESERVATION

MARBLE GORGE

PRIMITIVE ROAD

KAIBAB PLATEAU

N

Point Imperial

Mount
Hayden

Nankoweap Creek

Vista
Encantadora

Kwagunt Creek

Bright Angel
Point

Atoko
Point

Gunther
Castle

Little Colorado R.

WALHALLA PLATEAU

Cape Solitude

Shiva
Temple

Buddha
Temple

Bright Angel Creek

KAIBAB TRAIL

Deva
Temple

Angels
Window

PAINTED

Isis
Temple

Venus Temple

DESERT

Brahma
Temple

Cape Royal

Apollo
Temple

Phantom
Ranch

Zoroaster
Temple

Wotan's
Throne

GRANITE
RAPIDS

FOOT BRIDGE

KAIBAB TRAIL

Vishnu
Temple

Comanche
Point

Monument
Creek

Hopi
Point

GRANITE

Vishnu Creek

Pima
Point

Cedar
Mountain

Hermits
Rest

GRAND CANYON
VILLAGE

Yaki
Point

GORGE

Colorado River

Watchtower

Visitor Center

Lipan Point

Tusayan
Museum

Grandview
Point

Moran Point

0   5   10

MILES

DATE DUE

30 505 JOSTEN'S